WILD COMPANY

*The Untold Story
of Banana Republic*

MEL AND PATRICIA ZIEGLER

SIMON & SCHUSTER

New York   London   Toronto   Sydney   New Delhi

Simon & Schuster
1230 Avenue of the Americas
New York, NY 10020

First Simon & Schuster hardcover edition October 2012

SIMON & SCHUSTER and colophon are
registered trademarks of Simon & Schuster, Inc.

Credits for photographs and illustrations appear on page 209.

For information about special discounts for bulk purchases,
please contact Simon & Schuster Special Sales at
1-866-506-1949 or business@simonandschuster.com.

The Simon & Schuster Speakers Bureau can bring authors
to your live event. For more information or to book an event,
contact the Simon & Schuster Speakers Bureau at
1-866-248-3049 or visit our website at www.simonspeakers.com.

Designed by Ruth Lee-Mui

Manufactured in the United States of America

1   3   5   7   9   10   8   6   4   2

Library of Congress Cataloging-in-Publication Data
Ziegler, Mel.
Wild company : the untold story of Banana Republic   /   Mel and Patricia Ziegler.
p.   cm.
1. Ziegler, Mel.   2. Ziegler, Patricia.   3. Banana Republic Travel and Safari
Company.   4. Clothing trade—United States.   5. Fashion merchandising—
United States.   I. Ziegler, Patricia.   II. Title.
HD9940.U6B369   2012
381'.456870973—dc23   2012030040

ISBN 978-1-4516-8348-6
ISBN 978-1-4516-8351-6 (ebook)

For Zio and Aza

In the beginner's mind there are many possibilities, but in the expert's there are few.

—SHUNRYU SUZUKI

CONTENTS

CONTENTS

Wild
Company

The Racket Begins with a Jacket

NEWS MEDIA

SFPD
19 75

Mel Ziegler
Name

S.F. CHRONICLE
Agency

PASS THROUGH FIRE & POLICE LINES

Donald M. Scott

✷ CHIEF of POLICE, San Francisco Police Department

If you took 1,500 one-dollar bills and laid them end to end, they would stretch all of 750 feet. That gets you only three-quarters of the way down a crosstown block in Manhattan. We had to stretch those dollars into a lifetime—a lifetime free of ever having to work for anyone other than ourselves again.

I was a writer in my early thirties, and Patricia, several years younger, an artist. Newly in love, not wanting to be apart for a second, we itched to travel and see the world. That was never going to be possible if we continued to live month to month. We had met at the *San Francisco Chronicle,* where I worked as a reporter and Patricia as an illustrator and courtroom artist. The *Chronicle* job served up some stimulating opportunities for a young reporter in the 1970s, and I jumped and cajoled my way into as many as I could. I wrote several stories exposing notorious cult leaders (and questionable gurus such as Werner Erhard, the founder of est) then flourishing in San Francisco's fertile permissiveness, covered the charismatic philosopher Alan Watts's Zen funeral and the Patty Hearst kidnapping by a strange group called the Symbionese Liberation Army, interviewed Andy Warhol and other cultural icons, and wrote the first profile on California's eccentric new young Zen-spouting governor named Jerry Brown. Even so, many of my best ideas were rejected by editors for reasons that had nothing to do with the quality of the idea. Budget, for instance. As the joke went, a notoriously stingy management considered venturing across the Bay Bridge to Oakland to be an out-of-town story subject to layers of approvals. A union shop—every reporter hired was required to join and pay dues—the prevailing mentality in the city room favored seniority over initiative. Plum assignments went to tired old-timers who hacked out stories between swills of Jack Daniel's at Hanno's, the dive in the alley behind the Chronicle Building. If I happened to sneak a good story past the city editor and into the paper one day, I was punished the next day by being handed a pile of obituaries to write. I knew I had to get out of there.

It was an eventful time in San Francisco, and working at the *Chronicle* was exciting. I'd jump on the cable car to work, and many long nights would be spent in lively conversation with our colleagues and politicos at the Washington Square Bar and Grill, the North Beach media hangout. As a sketch artist in 1975 and 1976, I was assigned to cover the trial of Patty Hearst, the kidnapped newspaper heiress turned bank robber, and the trial of Sara Jane Moore, for the attempted assassination of President Gerald Ford. Thrilling as it was to see my work published on page one the morning after I sketched it, there was much downtime between such assignments and a lot of grousing from our colleagues about management, wages, and one another. Of the fifty or sixty people working in the city room, many of them our friends, most had been there considerably longer than we had— some even for twenty or thirty years. Not going to happen to us, we adamantly agreed. I started taking on freelance magazine assignments to fill the lulls, hoping I could soon be able to live on this work alone, trading in the day job for what appeared to be freedom.

One day I came home from work and shot Mel a playful I've-got-something-to-tell-you look. He had returned from an earlier shift and was on the couch reading.

Looking up, he asked, "What?"

"Guess what?" I could not wait to tell him. "I just quit!"

"No!" he replied impishly. "I was going to surprise you—so did I."

We were counting on freelance magazine assignments to tide us over until we figured out what to do. First we downsized, moving from our two-floor San Francisco apartment on Russian Hill to a two-bedroom house off Highway 1 in Mill Valley. The cars whizzed by at night, their headlights penetrating our blinds and invading our sleep. Magazine stories paid well but were irregular. Mimicking our moods, Indian summer gave way to a particularly long, cold, and rainy winter. The rough-sawn red-wood interior walls of our rented house kept the days dark. We knew we had to find a way out. While many of our journalist colleagues had invested their union salaries in Marin County houses when they were selling for less than six figures, we were barely making the rent.

We weren't panicking—we were too young and optimistic for that. We were interested in money only so it could buy us the freedom to paint, write, and travel. We didn't spend much. Our entertainments were hiking, biking, reading, and home-cooked meals with friends. Mel drove an old, beat-up Volkswagen, and I, an old Datsun. Even our cats were frugal, living off the local birds for their meals. We didn't dream about a "someday" with a house, children, and vacations in Hawaii. We viewed the future as one big, mysterious, open-ended possibility, which was what we had wanted, but our new circumstances were beginning to crimp. Freelancing, it became clear, wasn't so free.

Mel came home from the library one afternoon with a copy of Napoleon Hill's *Think and Grow Rich* and tossed it to me.

"Maybe this is what we need to do," he said.

The book prompted three basic questions: How much money do I want to make? How long do I give myself to make it? How will I make it?

We wrote down our answers separately and compared them. We had both scribbled "a million" and "five years." In 1978, $1 million was a number that any twentysomething middle-class American might have dreamed of making. Five years was the longest period we could envision. That both of us had come up with the same number and time frame validated our answers. Then we each looked at what the other had jotted down as an answer to the "how" question. Again, the same: "start a business."

But what business?

Several rainy days later, we had yet to find a business idea. The phone rang with a welcome magazine assignment for Mel to explore Australia with several other journalists. "It's probably just a junket," he said, "but it'll pay a couple of months' rent." While Mel went off to the sunny Southern Hemisphere, I braved the next few weeks home alone finishing up my local fashion column and putting the final touches on a magazine assignment about mail-order clothing.

Toward the end of the Australian junket, I wandered off one day into the backstreets of Sydney and stumbled on a "disposal store," which is what Australians call their surplus stores. I had been drawn to military surplus clothing since my days as a college student in the 1960s. Like others of my generation, I liked to wear surplus clothing because it was cheap. I also got a tickle from the paradox of being stridently antiwar yet happy to attire myself in military detritus. Until I stepped into the Sydney disposal store that day, most of the surplus I'd seen was originally issued to American soldiers. I was thrilled to find for the first time other surplus from Australia, Britain, France, and elsewhere. One item especially caught my fancy: a British Burma jacket. Made of thick but soft khaki cotton twill, it looked like a safari jacket. It had the tailored feeling of a fine garment. I had to have it, if only to wear it when I landed in San Francisco the following day. I wanted to see Patricia's reaction.

Patricia had exquisite taste and a limited budget, a dichotomy she balanced with a talent for spying gems at flea markets and vintage stores. Most people looking at her thought she'd maxed out the credit card on Madison Avenue, when she'd put herself together for pennies. I never thought much about clothing, which led to playful repartee between us. I needled her for being a fashionista, contrasting myself as someone who couldn't care less about what he wore. I claimed to dress in the "first available" clothing I found in my closet. But she was too smart to accept my preposterous claim, countering nimbly that I had *selected* every piece of clothing in my closet.

"Everyone thinks about what they wear," she said, laying me bare, "even people like you who claim they don't."

Walking jauntily out of customs at San Francisco International Airport in my new British Burma jacket, topped off with an Australian bush hat I also bought in the disposal store, was meant to be a playful concession to her irrefutable point.

A tan man in a khaki bush jacket and an olive green wide-brimmed hat pinned up on one side strode out of the glass doors of customs. I almost didn't recognize Mel. He'd been gone two weeks, the longest we'd been apart since we'd met over two years earlier. I saw him anew. My heart quickened as I watched him, with his usual intensity, searching for my face in the waiting crowd—and then our eyes met. He looked great. Our embrace knocked off his hat, an authentic Australian Army bush hat with the official puggaree band and medallion, he was quick to point out. But it was not his hat that most intrigued me. It was the jacket. How perfect the color, the raised lines of twill, the slightly worn collar and cuffs. This four-pocket jacket screamed "authentic" and "adventure." He caught my stare.

"Like it?" he said with a grin.

Driving home, Mel regaled me with stories of the Outback and the Great Barrier Reef, but my eyes kept drifting from his face to the jacket. Something was different. Had he acquired this new worldliness, this rather heroic nonchalance, from his adventures Down Under, or was it the jacket?

I had been fascinated by the transformative power of clothing since my first job at sixteen in a department store in downtown San Francisco. Visually starved by a childhood of Catholic school uniforms, I ravenously studied the dressing habits of the clientele from the more sophisticated side of the city. It became clear to me that sartorial habits communicated as much as Professor Henry Higgins discerned from accents. I began to understand how clothes conveyed character, charisma, and class, and with a newly refined eye, I picked out treasures lost in the bins of secondhand stores and flea markets, making slight alterations when necessary, to stretch my small clothing budget. Mel's new jacket said with panache close to everything that I and the friends I admired valued in life: character, adventure, heritage, and independence, especially from the frivolous dictates of fashion. However, it could use some new buttons.

Mel trusted me with the improvements. I added suede elbow patches and leather trim on the cuffs and collar, and swapped the metal military buttons for wooden ones. He loved the jacket even more and thanked me profusely.

"My favorite jacket of all time," he said, and he wore it almost every day.

With Patricia's classy refinements, the bush jacket became my proudest possession. Never had I been more at home in a piece of clothing. The jacket had an alchemical effect. I felt roguish and buoyant. Wearing it, I seemed to walk taller, with a more worldly gait. Everywhere I went, people stopped me with a comment or question.

"What a great jacket!"

"Where did you get that fabulous jacket?"

"Excuse me, do you mind if I ask you where you bought your jacket?"

On and on and on.

The jacket had a message for me, and it didn't take me long to get it: here was the business we'd been looking for. Patricia got the same message on her own. Yes!

Between us, we had $1,500 in our bank accounts. We would use it to start a company that would sell jackets like the British Burma jacket and anything else like it we could find.

Therein lay the full and complete business plan of a writer and an artist who had quit their jobs to make it on their own.

"What should we name it?" Patricia wondered.

That didn't take me a second.

"Banana Republic" popped into my head the moment she asked. What better proverbial source of military surplus than politically unstable tropical countries? I fantasized that routine coups produced an abundance of disposed uniforms from toppled regimes.

I could not have been happier. The name was not only catchy, but in 1978 it was jarringly irreverent as well. If years in journalism taught me anything, it was to grab 'em and get their attention. It was easier then. The era of fanciful company names spawned by dot-coms had yet to dawn.

The name was the easy part.

Starting a company wasn't so easy. Neither of us had any experience in business or had taken even a single business course in college. We knew nothing about retail, nothing about mail order, nothing about manufacturing, nothing about surplus, nothing about finance, nothing about management. The only asset we had was our own oblivion. That would keep us blissfully ignorant of the bewildering and arbitrary impediments that would entangle us until we became so embroiled that quitting was no longer a possibility.

As any reporter would, I began making phone calls. I learned that when the U.S. government declared military goods surplus, everything went to auction. I tracked down the next nearby auction at Travis Air Force Base in Fairfield, California. There the auctions were divided into "lots" into which government bureaucrats dumped all kinds of goods in no sensible order. A lot might contain "27 typewriters, used; 1,500 tubes of U.S. Army toothpaste, new; 2 F4F Wildcat propellers, used; four Jeeps' windshields, used; 724 pair of khaki shorts, size 42, used," and so on. If you wanted the shorts, you had to take the toothpaste too. For this reason, most of the bidders tended to be "jobbers," who were essentially junk dealers. They pulled up the truck, loaded the pallets, and pawned off the pieces to whomever and wherever they could. A few more phone calls, and I learned the names of the top six jobbers in the United States. One of them was right over the bridge in Oakland.

His name was Zimm, short for Zimmerman. I learned he had a huge warehouse overflowing with military surplus piled floor to ceiling.

I sensed that if we walked in cold, Zimm would not know what to make of us. In spite of our company name, I doubted that we could pose as insurgents looking to outfit threadbare comrades. More seriously, we didn't own a surplus store or have any pedigree in the surplus world. We needed a plan. Patricia devised one: we would pose as rich dilettantes. She would wear an expensive-looking dress and her highest heels to convey the impression that she was a trust fund heiress looking for "some interesting pieces" to supplement a boutique she was about to open. I would be the indulgent husband.

The visit became a strolling poker match, as the three-hundred-pound Zimm waddled behind us through the dimly lit, cavernous warehouse. It smelled like a mix of wet cement and rotting remainders of sandwiches. Occasionally he drew our attention to "goods" he was willing to part with at "a good price, depending on the quantity." It seemed as though we were wandering in a dark sepia photograph among brown, tan, and gray-green cloth mountains rising up from the cold, damp concrete floor. We could feel Zimm straining to size us up in the long silences.

So much stuff was packed into bins and piles that it was difficult to get a good look at what anything was. I asked him about

British Burma jackets. He'd seen them but didn't have any. Instead he pointed out piles of used combat boots, bales of new-issue nonwrinkle polyester shirts, woolen U.S. Army mittens, fatigue caps, plastic tarps, rope, mosquito netting. Each time, we nodded and moved on.

Now and then Patricia would pick up an item, feel the fabric, examine a detail, ask the price. The first two items she asked about were $2.50. She didn't react. The next few items were $2.00. She shrugged her shoulders, barely. We then came upon a huge pile of khaki shirts.

"What are these?" she asked.

"Spanish Army shirts," Zimm said.

"You seem to have a lot of them," Patricia said.

That was the signal for me to take a closer look. The shirts had epaulets. The fabric was finely woven. There was an exotic parachute emblem on the sleeves.

"You can have them for $1.75 if you take them all," Zimm said.

We haggled and settled at $1.50 each. The car loaded, we drove home to Mill Valley, half of all our money in the world invested in five hundred used Spanish paratrooper shirts stuffed in the trunk and piled to the ceiling on the backseat.

2

The Lady Closes the Deal

When we unloaded the shirts into our house, the fetid clues we'd been inhaling all the way home proved true. The shirts had not been washed since the Spanish paratroopers took them off. The Chinese laundry we frequented in North Beach was out of the question. It would charge more to launder the shirts than we paid for them. The only economical solution was to wash them ourselves, a load at a time.

We finished only a few loads before we had to take a

break and prepare for a long-arranged dinner party scheduled that night at our home. Our friend Herbert Gold, the novelist, was one of our guests. When Herb asked the way to the toilet, we directed him downstairs to the only bathroom in the house, which happened to be next to the washer-dryer. A few minutes later, he rushed back up the steps, beaming a broad, impish smile, and interrupted the patter at the dinner table by presenting, as a matador might hold up a cape, one of the Spanish paratrooper shirts.

"What is *this*?" he demanded in his deep baritone voice.

I told him.

Had I said it was the shirt Ernest Hemingway himself had worn while covering the Spanish Civil War, I don't think he would have been happier.

"I want one," he said. "How much?"

The words "Take it, Herb, it's yours," were about to come off my lips when Patricia interjected:

"Six fifty."

But he's our friend, my eyes pleaded across the table. Her eyes brushed me off.

"Plus tax," she added sweetly.

Banana Republic was born.

An exultant Herb took off his trademark denim shirt and put on his new Spanish paratrooper shirt right in front of us. We were all smiling until he slipped his arms into the sleeves. The cuffs fell well above his wrists. Patricia ran downstairs to get him another, but the sleeves on that shirt were also too short. And another, and another, and another. Every single one of the shirts was the same. *So this is why the Spaniards had declared them surplus,* I thought.

By this point, nothing was going to deter Patricia.

"Nobody would think of keeping the sleeves on a shirt like this rolled down, Herb," she said with an almost scary authority, rolling them up for him until they rakishly clung to Herb's elbows. She stood back, touched a finger to her chin, and nodded her head to show how pleased she was.

Herb caught a glimpse of himself in the mirror.

"Fabulous!" he declared.

Six miles from San Francisco, off the 101 freeway, is Marin City, where every Sunday a huge, dusty lot was transformed into a thriving flea market. We would sell the shirts there, we decided. Over the next few days, we washed, ironed, and folded every one of them. Sunday morning, off we went, sign in hand:

Short-Armed Spanish Paratrooper Shirts $6.50

There was no lack of curiosity. Many people stopped to touch the shirts and ask about them, but by the end of the day, we'd sold barely enough to pay the $30 booth fee.

We had a problem.

A *Chronicle* paycheck flashed in my mind for a second, though I knew I could never go crawling back there.

Patricia had a better solution. "We need to double the price," she said. "The shirts are too cheap. People can't appreciate the value."

The next Sunday, we went back to the same flea market. This time Patricia herself wore a Spanish paratrooper shirt belted at the waist with tight jeans and heels. She also dressed me in one with the collar slightly raised and the sleeves, of course, rolled up. Same table, same spot, same everything except the sign, which now read:

Short-Armed Spanish Paratrooper Shirts $12.95

It was a new day. By the end of it, we sold more than a hundred shirts. One hundred and two to be exact. Times 12.95 equals *one thousand three hundred and ninety dollars*. We had a good laugh. No one would ever believe us.

We decided to fast-track. It was time to graduate from flea markets. With more than $1,000 in the bank, Banana Republic needed a store.

I knew a real estate agent in town. Sure enough, he had a spot in our price range—if we didn't mind something a little unconventional. He showed us a four-hundred-square-foot space a few blocks from downtown Mill Valley. The rent was $250 per month. The unconventional part? The store had to remain unlocked at night because there was an aikido studio upstairs with classes at all hours, and the students needed access to come and go through the store space. "But they're honest," the agent said.

We took it.

It was early November. We made a list of the things we would need to do:

1. Find merchandise. We had only around 390 Spanish paratrooper shirts remaining, and besides, even we knew you can't have a store that sells only one item.

2. Print a catalogue. This might have seemed a bit excessive for our budget, but being an artist and a writer, we needed the comfort of doing at least something we knew how to do. Also, we must have realized that if we had any chance of selling this stuff, we'd have to explain what it was. I'd write the catalogue, and Patricia would draw it.

3. Decorate the store (though there would be little money left to do it).

4. Make a sign and hang it.

The more we thought about it, the catalogue struck us as key to the whole endeavor. What we were doing was unlike anything we'd ever seen in retail, and people would need a little help from us to catch on. Otherwise, who knows, they might think we sold bananas.

Oh, and that presented the next problem to be solved . . .

5. What exactly was the concept again?

3

Twists and Terms

Who could have known that $1,500, no matter how far we stretched it, wasn't going to make it? Not when you added up buying all the merchandise, paying the rent, fixing up the store, and getting a catalogue in the mail.

We figured we needed another $1,500 at least.

Perhaps *figured* is too precise a term. Since we had little clue as to what anything would actually cost, it was the number that "sounded right." We crumpled up the napkin on which we'd been jotting calculations and stopped guessing.

It was time to pay a visit to the bank where we had deposited our *Chronicle* paychecks over the years. The manager, Fred, was a pleasant man with red hair and an easy demeanor. I handed him the business card we had printed for the occasion and told him we had come for a loan for our new business. He looked at the card.

"Banana Republic?" Up went Fred's eyebrows. "Really?"

I nodded.

"And why the red star?" Fred asked.

He thinks we're Communists?

"I thought it went well with the yellow bananas and green leaves," Patricia replied, as any designer would. "It's meant to be a crest."

His thin smile came slowly, with evident effort.

Fred asked: Did we own a home? *No.* Did we have a business plan? *Working on it.* Did we have a regular source of income? *Not since we left the* Chronicle.

"I see," he said, nodding.

A kind man at heart, he proceeded gently. "To make a loan, we look at your three *C*s: Capital, which is your collateral. Capacity, which is your income. And Character. You have no collateral. You have no income. But I'll hand you this: you two *are* characters."

We must have looked like two sad puppies. He found a bone he *could* throw us.

"Look, you don't qualify for a loan," he suggested, "but have you thought about asking for terms from your suppliers?"

Patricia and I looked at each other. No, we hadn't.

"Net thirty is typical," Fred offered. "That means your

supplier gives you thirty days to pay. It's common practice in established businesses. Doesn't hurt to ask; you never know. Good luck."

Thirty days' credit would do just the trick, we decided. It would give us a chance to get the store stocked and open, put a catalogue in the mail, and start selling before we had to pay. All we had to do was talk Zimm into giving us terms.

But if terms were "common practice" and we hadn't even thought to negotiate them in our initial transaction, why would Zimm take anything less than cash on the spot from us now? I decided the best plan would be to get somebody else to give us terms first. Only then might we have a chance to talk the tough old geezer into doing the same. I remembered that at one point Zimm had asked me, "Where else you been?" Instinctively, I knew it would be a bad idea to tell the truth and say, "Nowhere." I just shrugged in a way that implied "Around."

"Well, let me give you a piece of advice," Zimm blustered. "Don't buy anything from that swindler Shapiro* in Sacramento.[†] "I don't trust that son of a bitch as far as I can throw him. I haven't talked to him in ten years."

Leaving the bank, we headed to Sacramento to find Shapiro. His warehouse was smaller than Zimm's, but the piles of surplus were arranged on shelves in an orderly fashion, and the lighting was better. Nonetheless, Shapiro's prices were higher, and the items he had in stock were mainly U.S. issue and not

---

*Not his real name, to protect him from questionable ignominy, considering the source.

†And not really here, either.

that interesting to us. However, we did find some old leather belts in a box stenciled with an address in Argentina, as well as a few Swedish gas mask bags, minus the gas masks, and some American M16 field jackets in good enough condition to sell. We haggled and reached the best deal we could.

"How you paying?" Shapiro asked as he finished writing the invoice.

"We usually pay net thirty," I said.

"You got a D and B?" Dun and Bradstreet is an agency that provides credit information on businesses.

I was still formulating an evasion when Patricia rejoined, "The family prefers not to reveal its assets."

"So who else you buy from, then?" Shapiro asked.

"Zimm," we both said at the same time.

"That stingy bastard gives you credit?"

We both nodded solemnly.

"Well, okay, thirty days, sign here."

Now we were ready for Zimm.

I had imagined there would be more great stuff in Zimm's sloppy bins than there was. The more we dug, the more I suspected we were unlikely to find any other items as good as the Spanish paratrooper shirts. Instead I found lots of unwearable items: arctic pant liners, mosquito nets, mattress covers, sleeping bag liners, and asbestos fire coats. I was growing discouraged, and then I realized that many of these discarded oddities were made of premium vintage fabrics. I could take them apart and make other wearable things from the materials. The fabrics themselves were treasures at below-bargain prices. This way we could get some more merchandise in time to open.

"I'll figure out something to do with this stuff," I whispered to Mel.

"You sure?" he asked.

"Like they say, when life hands you lemons, you make lemonade."

"So thirty days?" I said to Zimm when he added it all up.

"Your husband's got a sense of humor," Zimm remarked as he turned to Patricia.

"Shapiro gives us thirty days," Patricia said matter-of-factly.

Zimm glared at us. Then he unplugged the cigar from his mouth and discharged a burst of obscenities about his competitor.

We said nothing.

"Alright already," he agreed grudgingly. "Thirty days. And I don't mean thirty-one."

On the way home, we were so giddy that it did not occur to us that Zimm might be having the biggest laugh. He had unloaded on us a pile of otherwise worthless surplus that had been collecting dust for decades.

Finding Assets Hiding in Liabilities

There wasn't a minute to waste. We blocked out the windows of the tiny store on East Blithedale Avenue with butcher paper and went to work. We tracked down a few more dealers by phone, had them send us samples, establishing small "accounts" with any dealer who'd open one for us. Surplus dealers sold mostly to surplus stores, which specialized in hardy wear for hunting, fishing, camping, and other rugged outdoor adventures. What sold best in surplus stores were fatigues, military sweaters, jackets, hats, socks, and combat boots, all of it U.S. issue, in men's larger sizes. The stores didn't particularly care if the fabric was natural fiber or if an item had an interesting heritage, leaving a few gems for us.

Still, our best finds continued to be in the underlying fabrics. The bureaucrats who commissioned these items spared no expense in fabricating them in the highest-quality materials. There were Spanish Army sleeping bags with real sheepskin liners, British Army mattress covers made of pure Irish linen, French Army firefighter coats lined with exquisite quilted black satin, even ridiculous arctic pant liners made of a pricey windproof blend of wool and silk chenille. Since it seemed nobody else wanted this stuff, we often walked away with it for pennies.

There's an adage that journalists on deadline follow: *Go with what you've got.* And did we ever. We brought what we bought from Zimm back to the store and dropped it all on the floor to be cut apart and resewn into new designs. Fortunately, Patricia never lacked ideas. All we needed was a seamstress or two. A one-line help-wanted ad in the local paper elicited exactly one response. But she did the work of three. Her name was Anna.

She appeared like Athena, tall, dark, Sicilian, and silent. She brought with her an ancient black iron Singer sewing machine that I would soon learn held magical powers. I sketched, draped, cut, pinned; Anna sewed. This arrangement was sweetly familiar to me, having spent many contented hours as a child piecing together doll clothes from scraps of fabric on the floor while my

Italian mother and grandmother sewed clothing. Before long, the pile of surplus became Irish Linen Blazers, Basque Sheepskin Vests, Arctic Chenille Jackets, Black Satin Quilted Handbags. I also had Anna improve the few items we deemed possibly salable "as is." Dark green wool fatigue jackets were given new horn buttons and leather elbow patches. We sewed our red, yellow, and green embroidered logo onto caps, bags, jackets, and shirts. Some of the paratrooper shirts were combined to make Safari Dresses, to be worn cinched at the waist with ammo belts. Others were "disarmed," given a waistband and a second life as a skirt. We sewed our bananas-and-star-crest label into everything.

Lacking sewing skills, I began writing the stories for the catalogue that would have to sell this fast-mounting heap of khaki waste—or else. No longer did it represent only our life savings. By now we'd taken on a pile of debt, buying anything we could get on terms. Late at night, it sometimes hit us. If this didn't work, we would not just be broke but down there deep *below* broke.

The Tao of Averages

Rubes of retailing we may have been, but we had no illusion about one thing: our eclectic cache of surplus, no matter how much we cleaned it, altered it, and reinvented it, could not tell its own story. Websites hadn't even been dreamed up yet. Only with antediluvian moveable type and images could we get out the message.

I appointed myself Minister of Propaganda and went to work. However, this time in setting out to "go with what I got," I found there wasn't much "got" to go with, which put me in a position of having to go with what we didn't "got," such as the missing hoods on Italian camouflage jackets we'd found. On the back of the collar were prominent horn buttons for hoods that originally came with the jackets. Somewhere along the way, the hoods disappeared. In my copy I was left to conjecture about where they might be—still on back order from a factory in Turin that had been on strike since 1949.

Defects, I saw, could be worthy sources of inspiration. As for those short-armed Spanish Paratrooper Shirts, the time had come to expose a dirty little secret of history: Generalissimo Francisco Franco's paranoia of long-armed Spaniards.

So it went, Andalusian Militia Vests to Ammo Belts. I typed furiously, never missing a chance to dwell on what was wrong, what was missing, what made the item useless to the army or navy or air force that had declared it surplus. The few things I had an opportunity to write about that were new and in perfect condition were the kinds of things most people could not even conceive of needing—a crepe U.S. Infantry scarf, for instance. We renamed the scarf a Safari Ascot, as if anybody wore ascots on safari. The catalogue mused about the good gentleman buried in the bowels of the Defense Department who initially had requisitioned them. Dispatching infantrymen to the front lines in crepe ascots, he must have hoped, would fortify them with a touch of class in their bleakest hours.

As a writer and an artist feeling our way into business, we could take no chances. If customers didn't get the merchandise, maybe they'd buy the story. Thus, our dyslexia on the matter of assets and liabilities would be excused. We'd be able to pay for all the treasure we'd snatched on "terms."

While Mel wrote, I did a quick line drawing of each item. When all the copy and drawings were pasted down into hand-ruled boxes, our twenty-seven items filled two sheets of 8½" × 11" paper, both sides. For the cover and an order blank, we still needed one more side of a third sheet. This left one side, or two pages, blank when it was folded in half, to make a 5½" × 8½" twelve-page catalogue. Mel filled one page with his idea of an interview with me. On the other, I drew a cartoon telling our story "from the steamy jungles of South America to the icy wastes of Siberia . . ." even though we had yet to leave Northern California.

Next stop, the local instant printer, where we specified tan paper—two sheets regular, one card stock for the cover—black ink throughout, plus one color, sienna, on the cover only. At seventy-five cents each, we had enough money left to print five hundred copies but not enough to staple them. We figured we'd do that ourselves at our kitchen table.

Once we had the finished catalogue, we couldn't wait to get some reaction. We rushed over to see two friends who lived close by, a couple who were also writers.

We handed them each a copy. They stared at the leopard print cover. We beamed.

"Go ahead, read it!" Mel said as we plunked ourselves down on their sofa.

Quietly. Watching them. Turning the pages. We waited for laughs, smiles, wows. But when they finished, they looked first at each other and then at us. Uncomfortably puzzled.

"You don't expect this to sell anything, do you?" she asked, checking to assure herself that it was just a literary exercise.

He said, "You sure you want to mail this?"

Sure?

We left awkwardly.

"Do you think they might be right?" I asked Mel as soon we were out the door.

"No!" Mel said. "Absolutely not . . . or at least I don't think so."

"So . . . maybe?" I asked him.

"Look," he said, "it doesn't make any difference anyway, does it? We can't turn back now. It's as if we're swimming across the bay, and halfway across we realize there are sharks circling. We're no safer if we swim back than if we keep going to the other shore."

Failure was not a possibility. Not ever. The catalogue had to work, the store had to work, the whole idea had to work. There was no other way.

We hand addressed four hundred of the catalogues to everyone listed in both of our Rolodexes and as many people in the media we could think of or whose names we could get off mastheads. We licked the stamps and found a mailbox.

A day later, Mel came home with a book he had just found that was considered the bible of direct marketing. According to the bible, we had done just about everything wrong. We had no products in any of the traditionally high-yielding spots such as the cover, back cover, and page 3. Worst of all, based on our list of non-mail-order buyers, we could expect no more than an average 1 percent response, with an average order of 2.5 items. By those averages, we could expect to receive four orders of $30 each for a grand total of $120. That wouldn't even pay for the postage.

"What if what the book says about the averages is true?" I asked, feeling queasy.

"If we're average," Mel said, "we're screwed."

6

Going with What We Got

Even if we'd known axiom number one of retail, "location, location, location," we could not have heeded it. Our store at 76 East Blithedale Avenue in Mill Valley, at $250 per month, was already more than we could pay. It was situated on the ground floor of a two-story Tudor-style building, on the dark side of a side street two long blocks from the edge of the retail center of Mill Valley. In its prior incarnation, it had been the entrance to a 1960s head shop. The head shop had closed a few years earlier, and an aikido studio, run by former *Look* magazine editor turned human potential guru George Leonard, occupied the space.

Next door was a Laundromat, and on the corner, a small health food store. Our best hope was that we'd benefit from the foot traffic of people who were grocery shopping or doing their laundry. Perhaps they would need some safari clothes (we decided our sign would read SAFARI AND SURPLUS CLOTHING CO.). To catch the attention of drivers, I painted the door with a bold black-and-white zebra-skin pattern—heresy on the order of neon in this low-key town. Still, no one seemed to notice.

The funky knotty pine walls, which our lease dictated would remain unpainted, and the low ceiling, kept the space dark even when all the lights were on. The ceiling, which I covered with bright white butcher paper painted with a canopy of leaves, was supported by several old sawn-off immovable telephone poles. The chunky poles made it difficult to arrange our merchandise in a cohesive manner. "Going with what we got" (our mantra by now), I drilled holes near the top of each pole and glued in palm fronds from the flower mart to simulate palm trees. They were a bit stocky in the trunk but not altogether unconvincing. We painted the only Sheetrock wall, in the rear of the store, with leopard spots. We removed the interior shelves of a small closet and replaced its door with a curtain made from a camouflage tent, transforming the tiny space into a dressing room. Our largest expenditure was a floor-to-ceiling mirror on an eight-foot section of the side wall. In front of the mirror, we ripped out a grimy section of old carpet and replaced it with bright green Astroturf.

As soon as we took possession of the space, I submitted a sketch of our sign for approval to the fearsome Mill Valley Sign Commission, which enforced the town's lofty aesthetic standards by dictating the precise dimensions, shapes, and colors permitted for signage. By the beginning of Thanksgiving week, we still hadn't heard from them despite Mel's repeated calls. Mill Valley is a quaint small town, and we had been led to believe that the Sign Commission took its guardian role as a solemn oath.

Somehow even Mel and I knew that the day after Thanksgiving was the first day of the biggest shopping season of the year. Black Friday, as it has come to be called, was the day we planned to open. With only two days remaining, Anna was still sewing furiously. For extra last-minute help, I called my mother. She had a great eye and, conveniently, lived in San Francisco. The day before Thanksgiving, she walked into the store with an iron and two bags full of hangers. She took a look at the boxes and piles of khaki still spread all over the floor and said, "Okay, honey, what's the plan for all this?"

Uh-oh. In our rush to complete the merchandise, we had forgotten about display racks and shelves.

I remembered seeing some wooden fruit crates earlier that morning behind the Mill Valley Market. I asked and was told I could take them. Mel went in search of dowels and brackets at a hardware store. The dowels were reasonable enough, but the brackets cost more than $35 per pair, which eliminated them as a solution. "There must be something we can use," Mel said when he came back. I looked around and there was the box of old Argentine belts we'd bought from Shapiro, now dubbed "Gaucho Belts." We buckled a belt around each end of the dowel and nailed it to the ceiling. Perfect hanging racks. To complete the ad hoc displays, we tore the fruit labels off of the wooden crates from the Mill Valley Market, stenciled on the words "Imported from Banana Republic," and stacked them against the wall. We had shelving.

We worked late into the night and came back again on Thanksgiving morning to put things in final order. Somewhere around midafternoon, Mel went home to tackle the turkey. On his return, he found us scratching our heads over where to display the hats—the only new, nonsurplus merchandise that we had bought. We found them at a fifty-year-old hat company across the bay in Oakland. The styles included pith helmets, which worked perfectly with our assortment, and Humphrey Bogart–style fedoras. Mel grabbed a hammer and drove a series of long nails into the beams, and one by one hung a hat on each nail, the finishing touch that brought it all together. Except that the Humphrey Bogart–style fedoras, hanging up there on the nails, now looked distressingly new. The three of us pondered what to do for a minute or so, and then—*voilà!*—I pulled off the new, clean ribbon hatbands and replaced them with . . . Gaucho Belts! Now the hats oozed character and looked like they had just returned from a safari.

Only the sign remained to be hung.

"Have we heard from the Sign Commission?" Mel asked.

I told him we hadn't.

"We can't open without a sign," he said.

"What are we going to do?" I asked. "The sign needs to be approved."

"No problem," said Mel. "I approve it."

He carried the ladder out to the sidewalk and hung the sign himself. By nightfall, the store was ready to open. We went home and enjoyed the turkey.

The next morning, Mel and I, dressed head to toe in our khakis, drove down to the store and opened. Everything was in place—perfect.

We waited, and waited . . . and waited. And waited. For the first few hours, even though people came and went from the health food store and the Laundromat, nobody came in. Finally, a man stuck his head in the door. We both exhaled when he entered. For a few minutes, he wandered around, asked a few questions, and picked up one of the Swedish Gas Mask Bags for $6.50, plunking down a $20 bill on the zebra-striped cashwrap we had built.

In that moment, we realized there was one more thing we'd neglected to get: a cash register.

Mel made change from his own wallet.

A few more people stopped in that afternoon. One asked, "Where is the Banana Republic?" and someone else said, "Oh, it's down by Costa Rica. My cousin went there on his vacation."

There were no other sales.

7

Tropics in the Cold, Hard World

If this was the busiest retail season of the year, we were in trouble. We had miraculously managed to get our merchandise cleaned, remade, tagged, hung, the store opened, and even the catalogue printed and mailed in three weeks, but the moment we opened the doors, thud.

Store traffic the first few days after Thanksgiving was next to nil. Pedestrians passing by either didn't notice the store at all or didn't bother to come in. Two deadlines were beginning to look insurmountable. The December rent had to be paid in less than a week, and the first invoices from our suppliers—our magic "terms"—would have to be settled in a few days. If we were late to pay Zimm and our other dealers, we'd lose our credit and would not be able to keep the store stocked. I'd barely slept since we signed the lease, working around the clock to get the store open and the catalogue in the mail. Now Mel wasn't sleeping at all. He was the worrier.

I kept assuring Patricia that there was no reason whatsoever to worry. I licked every last stamp and took the catalogues to the post office the evening before Thanksgiving. The reason we had yet to see a response, I told her, was that they were stuck in the Christmas mail. When the catalogues hit in a few days, orders would flood in. So what if people in Mill Valley didn't get what we were doing? Our friends in New York would open their mailboxes. *They* would love it.

Meantime, with nothing else to do, since Patricia was handling the nonexistent store traffic by herself, I made myself useful by nailing down all the necessary but boggling legal and accounting particulars of the company. We had no money to waste on lawyers and accountants. We'd hire them to clean things up when the money came in. For now, Mom and Pop Inc. would have to do.

The mental logistics required to sort out this byzantine stuff wasn't the kind of thing that came naturally to me. Filling out incorporation papers and forms was drudgery, but nonetheless I managed to stay awake long enough to get the necessary documents delivered to Sacramento. Mastering the difference between an invoice and a receipt took some doing. Library books were instructive on how to set up the accounting, but for now, we'd just put the money in the bank and leave the balance sheet–payables–cash flow–income statement busywork for future development. Computers? Forget it. Jobs and Wozniak were still tinkering in their garage.

I waited. For the next couple of days, I stood in the store from ten until six, waiting for someone to come in.

I tried to keep busy rehanging and rearranging the skirts, dresses, and sheepskin vests into ever-new displays. In any event, I had to do this anew each morning because before going home in the evening, I hid much of the merchandise. I didn't want to tempt aikido students who nightly used our unlocked store as a hallway to and from their classes upstairs. I also busied myself sweeping the sidewalk out front, straightening the stacks of bags, and aligning the credit card forms and catalogues behind the counter. Waiting, waiting. A double album of Ella Fitzgerald singing Cole Porter songs, which we had recorded because Mel and I loved the romantic lyrics, played again and again all day long and then played all night in my restless sleep. Cole Porter, zebras, palm trees, Swedish Gas Mask Bags, old army sleeping bags born again as sheepskin vests—it was dreamlike anyway. Mel and I kept assuring each other that it was just a matter of time, just a matter of time.

Now and then a passerby peeked into the window, but when I tried to catch his or her eye, I rarely got back more than a fleeting glance. Even though it was quite cold outside and the store was unheated, I opened the door to make it easier for people to fall in, fortifying myself against the cold with a sheepskin vest over a wool fatigue shirt over a sweater and a T-shirt, as well as wool pants, boots, and a beret.

And then a woman wandered in, full of interest and questions. She began talking about troubles she was having with her husband. I listened while she tried on almost everything in the store. A few hours later, she bought an Andalusian Militia Vest for $19.50.

What's going on in the world gets inside us, and what was going on in San Francisco at the time was casting a dark pall on the whole Bay Area. The Monday after we opened, San Francisco mayor George Moscone and a councilman, Harvey Milk, were assassinated by another councilman, a former police officer. The assailant, Dan White, later claimed he was crazed on Twinkies. The week earlier, after assassinating Leo Ryan, a Bay Area congressman who had come on a rescue mission, an outsized San Francisco character named Rev. Jim Jones led more than nine hundred followers of his religious cult to commit mass suicide on a brew of arsenic-laced Kool-Aid in the jungles of Guyana. It wasn't exactly an opportune time to start a whimsical company. But here we were.

Little by little, people trickled in. I chatted up everyone, not only because it was lonely being in there all by myself but also because I began to see that the longer someone remained in the store, the better the chance that she or he would buy something. When no one was in the store, I tried creative visualization, counting the hours we'd be open until we had to write checks to Zimm and Shapiro and the landlord, and then calculating how many vests, skirts, and shirts that translated to per hour. This exercise made me even more determined never to let anyone who came through our door leave empty-handed. Even if they left only with a $6.50 beret or a Gaucho Belt, they were buying into our store. They were our best chance to get out the word.

Our first catalogue order came from a man in Bend, Oregon. I have no idea how he got the catalogue, since I hadn't mailed it to him. I was so ecstatic at the sight of his check, I sent him, along with the Short-Armed Safari Shirt he ordered, a certificate embossed with our corporate seal appointing him Honorary Consul of Banana Republic in Bend, Oregon. I decided to appoint the first customer in every town to be that town's Banana Republic honorary consul.

When the phone rang that first week, it was usually a wrong number. But in our circumstances, even wrong numbers were potential customers. I never let a caller hang up the phone without first informing him that he had just won a free Banana Republic catalogue, which I then promptly mailed if he gave me his address. But this time, it wasn't a wrong number. It was a woman asking to speak to the proprietor. She had noticed the unusual sign above the zebra-striped door.

I winced, put my hand on the receiver, and whispered to Mel, "It's the sign commissioner!"

But it wasn't the sign commissioner. It was Joan Lisetor, a reporter for the countywide daily newspaper, the *Marin Independent Journal*. Could she bring a photographer by and interview us about our unusually named company? She arrived later the same afternoon. Mel and I answered her questions. The photographer snapped a few shots.

It was Tuesday. We had enough money to meet the rent due Friday, but coming up with the $2,000 we owed Zimm less than a week later would take divine intervention. Early that Saturday, Mel and I went to the store. There was a crowd milling outside the door! A woman, seeing that I was puzzled, held up a copy of the *Marin Independent Journal*.

"Haven't you seen this?" she asked.

There it was: a full page—an entire page!—the front page of the Living section, with huge photos of Mel and me dressed head to toe in all the clothes we were selling in the store. The story began, "From the steamy jungles of South America to the icy wastes of Siberia . . ."

8

In Surplus We Trust

Patricia cut to the front of the line and opened the door. The waiting folks swarmed into the tiny space. I watched as they read the hangtags, sorted through racks, searched the shelves. They held things up in front of the mirror and waited their turn for the dressing room. Several people started piles on the counter. Then the credit cards and checkbooks began coming out. They didn't stop for the rest of the day and the day after.

Patricia stationed herself on the floor, refolding and finding sizes, while I was at the register grabbing the loot. Questions came from all sides:

"Does this come in any other colors?"

"Are these men's or women's?"

"Are the sleeves this short on all of them?"

Patricia was everywhere at once: No, only khaki, but it looks great on you. Men's, but they look so chic belted on women. Yes, but the sleeves are meant to be rolled up.

Ka-ching, ka-ching, ka-ching!

The sight of Mel dressed head to toe in khaki, as he was in his picture in the newspaper, coupled with their own Hemingway complexes, inspired the men. Everything in the store except the Spanish Paratrooper Shirtdress was men's clothing. The women were perplexed at first, but the times—the late 1970s—were in our favor. A subtle shift in women's fashions, spawned by the decade's flourishing feminist movement, made menswear influential in the styling of women's clothing. I guided the women in the store along. As soon as I found the first woman willing to try on one of our men's shirts, I double-belted it on her, and the other women in the store took it all in. Soon a second woman came out of the dressing room, laughing at herself in oversized men's pants. I was quick to cinch them with yet another two Gaucho Belts.

"Those look amazing on you," I said, and meant it. The khakis, oversized and masculine, emphasized her delicate frame and were surprisingly slimming.

Several husbands or boyfriends, themselves busy trying on pith helmets and safari hats, gave nods of approval.

By Monday, the shelves were looking bare, so before opening the store, we wrote out a check for the total we owed to Zimmerman and Sons, drove to Oakland, gave it to him (two days early), and went for another dig through the piles. Way down deep in the back, we unearthed brand-new shorts in bundles of twelve. They had wide-cut legs and buckles hanging off both sides of what looked like extremely wide waistbands that tapered into straps. The material was unmistakably the same fabric and the same deep khaki color of the British Burma jacket I had found in Sydney. Their labels: "British 1949."

Zimm said he had 1,500 and wanted $2.50 apiece. We must have betrayed ourselves, because despite our hemming and hawing, frowning, and head shaking, he would not budge on the price.

"What sizes are they?" Patricia asked.

"What sizes?" Zimm said. "Thirty-two, that's what sizes."

"Only thirty-two?"

"Thirty-two."

I took a breath.

"We'll take them all," Patricia said.

My brain went into the red zone, but I knew better than to doubt my wily and inventive wife.

"We'll need sixty days," I interjected.

Zimm threw up his hands in a mock gesture intended to convey, at great reluctance and against his better instincts, "Alright, already."

As the week passed into a new one, the newspaper story became history. Business slowly tapered off. The weather again grew cold and rainy, with frequent squalls. For the next few days, nobody came in the store for hours at a stretch. Some days there were no sales. Only the rare enthusiastic customer who got what we were doing with the clothing and the concept kept me going. Frustrated, chilled, and weary from standing in the freezing store day after day, I went home early one night for a hot bath and a glass of wine with Mel. Whenever we relaxed together, we traded assurances about how it would all work. I found my energy again and went in very early the following morning with ideas to rejuvenate the store by changing the window displays and creating a few new signs.

As I opened the door shortly after six o'clock, the phone was ringing. Wrong number, I assumed, answering "Banana Republic" with as much gusto as I could before my morning coffee.

"Good morning, Banana Republic! This is John Gambling live on WOR Radio in New York. You are on the air!"

That jolted me awake.

"Hello, John," I exhaled. The line crackled.

"I've just been reading to my listeners from your Banana Republic catalogue number one," John Gambling said. "Tell us more about how you find these unusual things."

Twenty minutes flew by in an instant as I, looking out the window at the driving rain, fielded one playful question after another.

"And tell us why there are no hoods on those Italian camouflage jackets?" John Gambling asked.

I recited Mel's catalogue copy, which by now I knew by heart.

At times I got carried away and went even further than Mel had in the catalogue. Where did we find the Spanish Paratrooper Shirts? We bought them by the pound in a back alley in Madrid.

"By the pound?" baited my interviewer.

"When the container arrived, we found some heavy old airplane parts buried at the bottom, packed in with the shirts."

John Gambling chuckled.

"Thank you Patricia of Banana Republic!" he said. "And if our listeners in the tristate area would like to get their very own copy of Banana Republic catalogue number one . . ."

He paused for a beat.

"All they need to do is send one dollar to post office box seven seventy-four in Mill Valley, California, nine four nine four two," I finished on cue.

The rain went on for another three days, keeping away shoppers, but on the fourth day, the postman came in dragging two massive sacks of mail from the post office across the street.

"These wouldn't fit into your box," he said wryly, "so I thought I'd bring them over."

That night Mel and I opened the envelopes. There must have been a thousand of them, each with a catalogue request—and a dollar bill.

Mel twinkled.

"What?" I asked.

"We not only have ourselves a business," he said, "we have ourselves a meal plan."

We grabbed a bunch of dollar bills and went out to dinner to celebrate.

9

Propaganda:
Handle with Respect

U p until we jumped into business, I wrote stories about other people. Suddenly things were different. I wasn't reporting the story anymore. I *was* the story. Banana Republic was the story. Seeing it from both sides of the reporter's notebook wasn't like looking into the mirror—it was being the mirror. As every journalist knows, you are only as interesting as your subject. As an entrepreneur, it was my job to be interesting. What reporter doesn't appreciate it when you help him do his job by being quotable?

Once John Gambling opened his WOR radio microphone to Patricia, media became the petroleum that powered our growth. Media loves media, and media is where media often goes to get story ideas. The more press we got, the more press we got. We happily played our part and accommodated each new media query with a press packet stamped "Propaganda: Handle with Respect" filled with all the other media stories. John Gambling had delivered us a marketing campaign we never could have bought.

Banana Republic's story landed on the chattering teletypes of the Associated Press, and newspapers everywhere scooped it up. All over America, readers were taking a last swig of their morning coffee and performing the ancient version of today's mouse click: finding a piece of paper, a stamp, a dollar, an envelope, and a mailbox to mail a catalogue request to a post office box number they had scribbled down.

Best of all, the ongoing deluge of catalogue requests generated lots of orders. All the books I'd read on mail order had made the same depressing point: up-front costs to get your catalogue into a customer's hands dictated that you'd lose money on the first orders. There was no possibility of a profit until you converted the customer into a repeat buyer. Yet we were generating orders at zero cost to us; the dollar sent with catalogue requests even covered the cost of the catalogue and the stamp. If I had read and followed the how-to books beforehand, I might still be collecting a paycheck at the *Chronicle*.

My serendipitous mail-order education got even more illuminating when a woman named Mary Lou Luther found us. She wrote a fashion column for the *Los Angeles Times*. She spotted and praised the 1949 Ghurka shorts. The *Times* pushed her column across its wires to scores of other newspapers from Maine to Arizona. These were the "size-32-only" shorts we had found in Zimm's musty coffers. We'd since learned the shorts had been issued to the Ghurkas, an elite Nepalese brigade employed by the East India Company who later served in the British Indian Army. But it was not their exotic lineage that charmed Mary Lou. She deemed the Ghurkas to be the single most chic short of the summer, fitting all men and women *up to* size 32, due to the adjustable waist, and told her readers where to send their checks to secure their own pair. For weeks afterward, the letters that flooded in no longer held just a measly dollar but checks for $15. Even better, with every pair of shorts, we sent the customer a catalogue in the box (called a "bounceback" in the mail-order parlance we were fast mastering). Many customers then placed additional orders.

AUTHENTIC BRITISH
GHURKA SHORT

Post repast adjustment (3"-4")

Deep Pockets for Deep Thoughts

Do as the British wouldn't dare: Roll up the cuffs

We worked late into the evening and sometimes all night to fill the tsunami of orders and to put together a second catalogue, which proved even more successful than the first. According to the mail-order experts, a good response was 2 percent, but we were getting more than 10 percent. We were starting to think maybe there was something to being accidental professional amateurs.

It would have been heartening if our promotional skills were matched by our operational skills. Since I was by nature impatient and therefore hopeless in the store ("Come on, lady, make up your mind!"), it became Patricia's turf. In between waiting on customers, she also took phone orders. Meantime, I cobbled together a Rube Goldberg system to process the mail orders. The accounting, the invoices, the back orders, the inventory, the shipping, the sales taxes or no sales taxes, the deposits, the credit cards—paper was flying all over the place. There had to be an easier way, but I was too overwhelmed just processing the business to figure it out. Patricia was overwhelmed tending to the store and keeping it stocked with fresh merchandise.

And then Tess Gowins walked in the store. Blonde hair worn in a burst of curls, lovely in every way, soft, faded flannel shirt belted over cutoffs, and long, tanned legs in cowboy boots.

"Are you hiring?" she asked Patricia.

"Do you have any retail experience?" Patricia asked her.

"No," she said, "I'm an artist."

An artist, no experience. Perfect.

"We can only afford to pay minimum wage," Patricia apologized.

"That's okay," Tess said. "I like your store."

"Can you start tomorrow?"

After a week, we promoted Tess to store manager, freeing up some of Patricia's time to tackle the other hundred-plus things on our to-do list.

With Tess on board and sales depleting inventory faster, it seemed like a good idea to take another crack at the military auctions and do some bidding ourselves. We headed up to Travis Air Force Base for the monthly auction. As we entered the massive hangar, a uniformed man handed us a mimeographed list on a clipboard and a bidder's number. He directed us to the pre-auction viewing area. What we saw was more than a little disorienting. Piles after piles of weird and preposterous "surplus" had been dumped in evenly spaced heaps along a concrete walkway. Each pile was cordoned off with a rope and marked with a huge number. It was impossible to make out exactly what was in each lot, but the mimeographed handout spelled out the contents in prosaic military-ese: "U.S. Army Fatigues, olive drab, size 46XL, new; Combat Boots, size 16EE, used," and so on.

"Bureaucracy meets merchandising," quipped Patricia.

Something in lot 79 caught my eye: white satin fabric ending in rib-knit cuffs. I tugged on a sleeve. It was attached to what seemed to be a jumpsuit.

I pointed for Patricia to have a look. She grabbed my arm and pulled me away.

"Don't act so interested," she whispered, pushing the clipboard under my nose.

Her finger pointed to number 79 on the mimeographed list: "Typewriter ribbon, black, 1 gross. Tarp-OD-20 x 40. NASA-05571 flight suit-4 dozen . . ."

Indeed—NASA flight suits!

We took our seats on the cold metal folding chairs in an audience of fifty or so dealers, some of whom recognized us. A few eyebrows went up.

The bidding started, and went quickly. After each lot sold, there was a bit of noisy squirming in the room, as the dealers did some fast trading among themselves. Then came lot 79.

"Do I hear one hundred?" called the auctioneer.

My hand went up.

"One hundred and fifty?"

No other hands.

"One hundred twenty-five? Do I hear one hundred twenty-five?"

Nothing.

"Sold for one hundred dollars!" boomed the auctioneer. Patricia squeezed my knee.

We unloaded our cache as soon as we got back to the store, pulling out the boxes of typewriter ribbons to get to the flight suits and their helmets tangled in yards of clear plastic tubing. Impatiently, I started cutting off the tubing to free the flight suits. But it was soon apparent why we were the only bidders. These *were* authentic flight suits indeed, but a little *too* authentic for our customers or anyone else who might entertain the idea of wearing one on terra firma. At the breasts and groin of each suit were large rubber gaskets where the tubes for oxygen and vital functions were attached.

"A hundred dollars down the *tubes*," Mel joked.

But wait a minute!

I remembered the failing American space station called Skylab that had been in the headlines almost every day. I had just read in a July 1979 issue of *Time* magazine:

The world this week awaits an unprecedented event: the fiery fall of the largest machine man has ever hurled into space. The American Skylab vehicle, nine stories tall and weighing 77.5 tons, is expected to slip into the earth's upper atmosphere, then disintegrate into a celestial shower of flaming metal . . . Somewhere . . . fragments, each weighing 1,000 lbs. or more, will crash to earth at speeds of up to 270 m.p.h. with the force of a dying meteor.

There was much discussion and more than a little panic about where Skylab pieces would fall. I grabbed the phone to call every local TV station. Banana Republic in Mill Valley had a limited supply of "Skylab Protection Suits" that it was selling on a first-come basis, I disclosed anonymously.

That night we were on nearly every local station at six and eleven.

Not a single flight suit sold, but the store was packed for two weeks afterward.

Pros and Cons

At the SOP (Seat of the Pants) School of Business, we took help wherever we could get it. Shortly after the Skylab incident, we exhumed Italian Army Bersaglieri shorts from the bins of a Brooklyn surplus jobber, Schwartzman. The Bersaglieri were an elite group of sharpshooters. After paying wistful homage to the bygone quality of the fabric and the expert workmanship in the shorts' construction, the catalogue mused, "Italians may not be much on the battlefield, but when it comes to style, they conquer all." The serendipitous law of unintended consequences elevated that throwaway sentence into a small international incident.

Who knows what odd chance brought the catalogue to the attention of the Italian consul in Los Angeles, but fate did, and he was insulted. He was outraged. He was fuming, and he was . . . right! Who were we to use our catalogue to disparage the Italian Army, which for all I knew (basically nothing) may have the bravest, most fearsome, formidable soldiers in the world? As his protest fed the airwaves beaming radio talk shows for hours one morning to commuting Angelenos, I cheered him on. He had no more fervent supporter than I, applauding his every righteously scornful word, so laden with . . . publicity! The incident brought us four times as many orders to fill as we had shorts, again confirming the adage "There is no such thing as bad publicity."

Thanks to one stroke of luck after another, the publicity kept coming as the catalogue found its way across America. The pace quickened by the day. I believed the best way to ensure our long-term survival was to *overdeliver.* Go above and beyond and, most importantly, make a human connection with customers. I scribbled notes to customers and put them in the boxes. The notes, on official khaki stationery, were signed by a random minister of the Republic: sometimes Minister of Finance, others the Minister of Progress, but usually the one truest to me, the Minister of Propaganda. I had stamps made to stencil sayings—"In Surplus We Trust," "One Man's Bush Jacket Is Worth Two Designer Jackets"—on the tissue paper in which we wrapped all orders. Nothing was too silly. Checks written to Banana Republic were stamped "Warning: contributions to struggling young countries are not tax deductible."

The publicity made it a challenge to keep the shelves stocked. At any given time, one or the other of us had to be out prowling dealer warehouses around the country while trying to juggle all of our other responsibilities. I was shipping foreman, mailing list coordinator, errand boy, accountant, window washer, legal counsel, floor sweeper, marketing guy, copywriter and president, not to mention husband of the co-owner, who herself was parallel drowning.

My territory was the visual realm: store design and display, clothing redesign, catalogue illustration and design, and the miscellaneous logos and graphics on our labels, T-shirts, bags, signs, business cards, and so on. I was also part-time salesgirl, janitor, laundress, bookkeeper, shipping clerk, vice president, and wife of a partner with a new idea every minute. Each morning, I'd iron the merchandise we'd washed the night before, sew on labels, write up hangtags, and on many mornings open the store by ten o'clock. In between waiting on customers, I wrapped and shipped packages, took phone orders, and tried to analyze our sales to see how much merchandise to buy. When I got home, there was more book work, banking, and endless laundry. We were perpetually running out of catalogues as well as merchandise. Our pillow talk was strategic planning.

Meanwhile, at the store, we were nearing the midterm on Retail 101.

With more store traffic and more store hours in a week than one employee could work, we were on the lookout for a second salesperson. As if on cue, Miss America came through the door asking for a job. Perfect teeth, perfect skin, perfect nose, perfect hair, perfect figure attached to a perky personality. Annette looked good in the clothes and said she had experience at a boutique back east. We hired her. For the first couple of weeks, she worked hard at selling, kept the store in good order, and closed out the register every day. The aikido studio had found a way to use a back staircase, allowing us to lock up at night, so we gave Annette a key for when she needed to open or close the store on her own.

One morning she called Patricia. Sobbing, she said we'd been robbed. She had found the door jarred open when she arrived, and "the box with the receipts" gone. The box, stuffed in a hiding place that only she, Patricia, Tess, and I knew, was where the cash, checks, and credit card receipts were held until we deposited them the next day. This particular day's receipts, now missing, represented one of the best days we'd had in a while.

Patricia: "Everything's gone?"

Annette: "Everything."

"Even the checks and credit card receipts?"

A beat, then: "Yes."

"I'll be right down," Patricia said, hanging up.

She headed for the door.

"What are you going to do?" I asked.

"Get it back."

When I got to the store, the door was locked. Annette wasn't there. I glanced around. The leather jackets were still hanging on the rack, and nothing else seemed out of place. I dialed Annette's home number. She answered.

"Where are you?" I asked.

"I didn't feel well, so I just came home," she said. "I was about to call."

"You need to take care of yourself, then. I'll check on you later."

I hung up and called the police. Nothing out of place, I told them, no signs of a break-in, only the day's receipts were missing, with a lot of cash sales. The police agreed that yes, she probably did it, but with only circumstantial evidence, there was nothing they could do.

"Here's the thing," said the officer. "You'll probably never see that cash again, but you could confront her and threaten to turn her in unless she gives you back the checks and credit card receipts." (Credit transactions were still years away from being transmitted electronically.) "But don't get your hopes up. If she's a pro, she won't fall for it."

I called Annette again, this time apologizing for bothering her when she wasn't feeling well, but said I needed to unload some heavy boxes from the van and could use her help because Mel was out of town. I offered to drive to her house and pick her up and then take her back home afterward and even bring her some soup from the market. She agreed hesitantly but said she could drive herself to the store. I met her in the parking lot and signaled for her to come into the back of the van with me. As soon as she did, I slammed the sliding door shut, locking us both inside.

Her face showed sheer terror.

"All right, I know you took the money, and the police know you took the money. There are fingerprints all over the place," I threatened in a tone so menacing I even scared myself. "All the police need me to do is press charges, and you're in jail."

She froze, confirming my hunch. The one-tenth of 1 percent of me that worried I might be wrong was relieved. I watched her mouth fall open, wordless.

"You should be locked up for this, but, frankly, I am so disappointed in you, I just want you out of my life."

She exhaled, eyes pleading.

I stared hard at her, then said, "What did you do with the checks and the credit card slips? If I get them back, maybe I'll consider not pressing charges."

"I threw them in the Dumpster over there," she blurted, bursting into tears. "It was my boyfriend who made me do it. Please, no police."

"Go get them! Now!" I demanded, opening the van door. She jumped out. I followed right behind as she headed to the Dumpster. She stuck her hand in it and rummaged around the top layer of garbage until she found the box and handed it to me, shaking. I checked it. No cash, but the credit card slips and checks were still there. When I looked up, she was already hurrying to her car.

You would have thought we were the Bank of America. Disguised felons kept coming to rob us. The friendly man in his thirties, well dressed in slacks, button-down shirt, and loafers.

Telling stories of polo matches, trying on a couple of leather jackets, more polo stories, thinking about this jacket or maybe that one, and then coming back on a Saturday afternoon when the banks were closed and writing a check for $850. When the check bounced, Patricia headed straight to the address on the check with a burly officer from the Mill Valley Police Department.

The officer had told her that he could not legally enter the man's apartment without a search warrant. But that did not deter Patricia. She persuaded the officer to come with her only for protection. He would wait outside; she would enter the apartment and get the merchandise back. The officer drove her to the man's apartment in a squad car, and accompanied her to the door. As it turned out, it was his boot stepping over the transom that prevented the thief from shutting the door in Patricia's face. She got the leather jackets back.

I never met the pros who flung a brick through the plate glass window in the middle of the night. They went for the leather jackets as well. On this occasion, I learned there were several pages advertising "24-hour Plate Glass Window Repair" services in the Yellow Pages. Welcome to retailing.

Ultimately, these incidents were bumps on the on-ramp, but they didn't feel like bumps at the time. They felt like crashes.

Details, Details

A few bruises, a little beat up, but on we went. The days began to blur, yet somehow we rented a desperately needed warehouse and hired a few clerks to handle the phones, type up the orders, and pick, pack, and ship them out.

The warehouse was a few miles away in Sausalito, near houseboats on the waterfront. Having honed my skills on stingy surplus dealers, I negotiated a great deal on a lease. Or so I thought.

"Remember now, this is the waterfront," the landlord said as we each signed. "Sometimes the tides get a little high."

That bit of deft circumlocution, I would soon learn, was meant to inform me that the warehouse would flood if it rained at high tide on full moons. So much for reasonable rent. A few weeks later, it rained on a full moon. The waters of San Francisco Bay swooshed in during high tide and covered the floor two feet deep. We figured we'd just go home and come back when the tide receded, but our cars were submerged as well. Fortunately, our eclectic inventory included surplus wader boots. We promptly donned them and passed them out to the employees. This became our ritual practice, allowing us to pack and ship mail orders without interruption during the hours of high tide whenever it rained on a full moon.

The warehouse flooding, easily navigated with our wader boots, turned out to be a relatively minor problem when measured against a more daunting predicament. We were building a market for a type of product that could not be reliably replenished. Jumping into the business, we had no choice but to buy whatever we could as cheaply as we could. The prospect that there would be nothing left to sell was not something we had the luxury of worrying about. But now it *was* a real problem. If we were as successful as we hoped, we could exhaust the world's vintage military surplus, most of which had been produced in the Second World War. It was the congenital flaw in our business concept.

The only solution, if it could even work, would be to produce our own line of clothing inspired by the best surplus. Under this scenario, we would feather in our own designs and sell them right along with the surplus as the surplus phased out. Any other path would guarantee extinction.

Of course, designing our own line and having it manufactured would take money—more money than we had. Not to mention how two inexperienced people already stretched in every direction were going to get it done. We were already using whatever remaining mental and physical energy we had to keep our business going from one day to the next, let alone next month or next year. Not only did we have a store to manage and run, but it was a store where all the merchandise had to be discovered, remade, or fussed with in some unusual way. And on top of that, we needed to feed a catalogue that had to be planned, produced, updated, analyzed, and fulfilled—mostly by us. We had unwittingly plunged into three businesses at once, each of which itself would have been a handful—a store business, a catalogue business, and a remanufacturing business—and all of it without money to back us up. Had we been a bit less impetuous at the outset, a little more planning might have simplified things. We didn't yet have so much as a system for tracking the value—or quantity—of our inventory. An item was either on the shelf to pick and pack, or it wasn't. If it wasn't, it could have been (a) sold, (b) shoplifted, or (c) pinched by an employee. We'd find out later. For now, we grabbed and hired all able persons who came through the door looking for a job, and fed them into a company whose systems and organization were challenged. While it helped to have a small pool of cash from store and catalogue sales keeping us afloat, the boat was leakier than ever, and we were in no less danger of capsizing.

I kept running notes on my bedside table of everything keeping me awake at night:

Problem 1. We need more merchandise and variety than the surplus dealers can offer, especially for women.

2. There is not enough time to remake surplus.

3. Our unusual merchandise takes work to sell, and the prices are so low that selling $500 worth is exhausting.

4. No matter how many new things we get, it is impossible to make the store look fresh and exciting because everything is always the same drab khaki or olive drab color.

5. Our washer and dryer are wearing out.

6. So are we.

In coming up with solutions, I worked backward as usual.

6. Wasn't going to be solved until the other problems were, so . . .

5. Easy! The Laundromat was next door.

4. This one troubled me most. Our whole business was based on khaki, and even I was getting sick of wearing it every single day. But as long as we relied on surplus, that's what we were going to get: shades of khaki, olive drab, and maybe a touch of navy and occasional white. Pucci we were not.

How we solved this problem was why our partnership worked. What one of us just couldn't deal with, the other took on.

On the afternoon of a rather stressful morning, Mel called me at the store from a pay phone on a noisy, windy corner in San Francisco.

"I know what you need to do!" he screamed into the receiver over the howling wind.

"What?"

"Diet!"

"Whaaaat?!!" I screeched back. *Oh my God! Is he actually telling me that I'm getting fat?*

"Di! It!" he yelled again.

"You're kidding, right? I don't even have time to eat anymore!" I tried to keep my voice down as a customer turned to stare. I was growing furious.

"No, no, no!" he laughed. "I mean *dye* the surplus. Where is it written it has to be khaki? Get some color into the store!"

Breakthrough! Natural fabrics would dye beautifully, and with khaki as the base, the boldest colors would take on the richness of a tinted photograph. We could dye wartime thermal underwear tops, khaki shirts, white cotton shirts, wool aviator scarves that had yellowed with age, and what I suspected would be the biggest hit of all: some funky World War II overalls we nabbed from Zimm for a song.

Yes! I thought. *I'll dye everything I can.* Then we'll deal with problems one, two, and three.

Jeito!

After dropping a new catalogue in the mail, and while waiting for it to hit (it took a few weeks when mailed economically at bulk rates), we decided to seize the lull for a vacation that we had been dreaming about ever since we met. We left our newly hired crew in charge, trusting they'd figure out what to do, and took off for . . . Rio!

Imagine a world without cell phones, e-mail, and Internet, in which international communications were expensive and often unreliable. And here we were leaving behind our business and flying down to Rio de Janeiro as insouciantly as Fred Astaire and Ginger Rogers.

To be free to do as we wished and to travel—that's why we had started this company, right?

Rio represented the ultimate fantasy of freedom to us: the freedom of living spontaneously in the day. It was hot, it was exotic, it was sexy, and it was cheap. After months of nonstop 24/7 days in our own Banana Republic, we wanted to play in someone else's. Brazil was the perfect ticket. We handed the keys to the employees and jauntily sambaed off. Our plan was to stay three weeks until the catalogue hit. We decided to rent an apartment in Ipanema.

As we walked into the first real estate office we found, a dark, lanky man in a white short-sleeved shirt got up to greet us and signaled for coffees. Three demitasse cups filled with dark coffee and melting sugar cubes arrived in seconds. Two swigs, and we rocketed off with the man to look at an Ipanema penthouse a bit more frayed than we would have liked. But it was in a great location and the right price. We took it.

We threw down our bags, changed into our swimsuits, and headed immediately for the beach. There we saw miles of beautiful bronze girls in tangas and guys in mini Speedos covering almost every inch of white sand except where fierce games of beach volleyball were in progress.

We found a place to wedge in and threw down our mat on the warm sand. Our bodies, frozen with more tension than we had realized, began to thaw in the Brazilian sun. What a great idea to come here, we agreed and kissed. I felt a tap on my shoulder and looked up to see a man in shorts babbling something in Portuguese. Having studied my Berlitz phrase book on the plane, I shrugged and said, *"Não falo Portugese."* He rattled on, frustrated. *"Não falo Portugese,"* I repeated. He could have cared less, as I was about to learn. I reached for my bag to get my sunglasses. The bag wasn't there. Looking up in sudden terror, I saw it on the arm of another man rushing away on the beach. I jumped up and chased him, yelling, but the man disappeared into the crowd.

Gone: passports, return tickets, credit cards, traveler's checks, and the rest of our cash. No! Suddenly we had nothing, no ID, no way back home. Nothing but a few cruzeiros left in my pocket and a key to the Ipanema penthouse we had just rented. I looked around at the unconcerned crowd.

We found our way to the nearest police station, and with the help of much gesturing and one policeman who understood some Spanish, we explained what had happened. They shook their heads, suppressing smiles.

"Is there any chance we'll get our bag back?" Mel asked.

The one who spoke *un poco de español* repeated the question in Portuguese to the others.

They all laughed.

Then they pantomimed what had happened. We nodded, and they laughed again.

The joke was that nobody with any sense would *ever* think of taking anything of value to the beach in Rio.

On our way back to our apartment, still digesting what had happened, we passed a newsstand where a large headline on the only newspaper in English screamed:

SAN FRANCISCO DESTROYED BY EARTHQUAKE

A few lines, no details. Nothing in any other newspaper. Nothing we could do about it anyway. (Turned out it was a mere 5.8 quake across the bay in Livermore, barely felt in San Francisco.) It was the end of the day. Barefoot crowds were walking back from the beach, talking, teasing, laughing, flirting, many heading back to the ramshackle favelas we glimpsed on the hillsides. Nobody carried a bag, only rolled-up reed mats and, at most, a cruzeiro note tucked into the side string of her bikini. Precarnival drumbeats filled the languid air. Occasionally a group of people broke into a samba on their way down the street.

At first their pleasure grated on us. But then as the city's ongoing party inexorably closed in around us, almost without realizing it, our gait loosened and our bodies began to sway. What *was* it about these Cariocas? Even though many clearly had next to nothing, they were unmistakably happy. Happier than most Americans we knew. Carefree. It was infectious.

Passing a samba school, packed with people dancing, we joined in. In a short time, we became mesmerized by the repetitive beat. We ended up at a wild nightclub, spent the few cruzeiros I had left in my pocket on a plate of rice and beans, and then danced in the streets with everyone else until we had only enough energy to stumble back to our bed.

The next morning, we went to seek advice from the only person we knew in town, the real estate agent.

"I have something for you," the man said as we entered, happy to see us. He handed us our bag. Tickets, passports, and wallets were there, but no credit cards, traveler's checks, or cash. But in Mel's wallet was the receipt for the traveler's checks. They could be replaced.

Dumbfounded, we asked him how he got the bag.

"You had my card in there," he said. "Somebody found it on the beach."

Three coffees arrived, so we sat down and told him about our night.

"Ah, you are learning about *jeito.*" He smiled proudly. "It's what keeps us Cariocas going." Roughly translated, it means "There is *always* a way."

When All Else Fails, Expand

When we got back, did we ever need *jeito*.
I'm not sure what we expected to find, but
it wasn't walking in the door and seeing a half dozen
chatty employees laughing and having coffee, oblivious
to piles of mail that had yet to be opened and orders yet
to be filled. When bulk mail will be delivered is always
unpredictable. This time the catalogue hit much earlier
than we anticipated. In the back room, the warehouse,
there were heaps and heaps of unopened boxes filled with

merchandise being returned from customers who had been sent the wrong items. Our newly hired warehouse guy had decided to improve the pick-pack-ship system in which I'd trained him. Instead of packing one order at a time, he batched the orders, put them all in boxes, and then, at the end, went down the line attaching all the labels, which "somehow" got a bit "mixed up."

That was just the start. The phones were ringing incessantly, far more than could be answered at any given time, with frustrated customers calling to place orders, or to ask where their orders were, or to complain about being sent the wrong stuff. Since all the lines were lit up, other customers behind them could only have been reaching busy signals.

It took Patricia and me more than a few gulps of *jeito* and weeks to clean up the mess. As much as we could.

Rio evaporated in a minute. Fixing the problems that occurred while we were away drained everything out of me. We wanted to put things right again. We gave it everything we had, all day long and every day of the week. "Failure is not a possibility" had been our motto all along, but with the post-Rio chaos, we came scarily close to a place where even the self-hypnosis of such mantras would not work. We both carried on. It would have been unthinkable for either of us to let the other down.

Nonetheless, by the time we got things back into a semblance of order, while Mel seemed to be still hanging on, I was beginning to crumble. Gone was a yoga practice that I had relied on for ten-plus years. Not enough sleep. Eating on the run. Too much coffee. No time for anything but keeping it all going. I was getting cranky, snapping at Mel. He was snapping back. We both knew that blaming each other was fruitless. We never ceased giving it everything we had, but for the first time, I began to question whether it was enough.

It was also becoming increasingly obvious to me that Mel and I were very different people. Mel was laserlike, searing right to the main issue, extracting the problem, and not letting it out of his grasp until he overcame it. My way was to sink in and absorb, trusting that the solution hiding in the problem would reveal itself to me. Where Mel paced in the overview, looking for how to rearrange things in a more workable order, I dug hands-on into the physical thick of things and worked my way out from there. That sometimes made me too slow for him. He could be too abstract for me. Usually we just ran on parallel tracks, and it didn't matter. We would each get our work done in our own way. At times, however, we'd collide, and those collisions were happening too frequently. It was getting downright dangerous. When you are friends, spouses, and business partners all at once, fighting not only shakes up the life you've built together but also upsets the whole world around you, draining it of hope and energy. Everything is at stake: friendship, family, marriage, career, self-esteem. Our fights could be loud and fierce, although they usually evaporated quickly, leaving both of us a bit embarrassed afterward. Ultimately, we agreed on the big issues, until . . .

A few months after the post-Rio debacle, one night after a final postmidnight press check at the printer's on yet another catalogue, having had no sleep the two prior nights, I was driving home. The blast of a truck horn startled me. I was drifting into the oncoming traffic on the Golden Gate Bridge, where only plastic cones serve as a middle barrier. I had fallen asleep at the wheel. Were it not for the truck horn, I might have died in a head-on collision. It was a turning point. I decided the catalogue was too much. I could not do it anymore. The store itself was more than enough to handle.

At breakfast the following morning, I told Mel firmly of my resolution. "We have to stop the catalogue. We've taken on too much."

He shook his head.

"We can't go backward," he said.

"Well, we can't stay where we are," I insisted. "I'm at my limit."

"I know," was Mel's cryptic response. "I've been giving it a lot of thought."

I looked at him and waited. He bit his lip. He looked at me, suppressing a smile.

"And? So?" I was not going to let it go.

"Our problem is that we're going in circles. We need to bust out, make a go for it."

"What? Bust out? How?"

"Open another store," he said.

"What?!" I was furious. "You're not hearing me!"

I got up to leave, angrily. Mel came after me.

"I do hear you," he said. "I've been thinking a lot about this. We need to scale up so we can get the help we need to make all this work."

He insisted that I take a few days off, all to myself, "even if it means things falling apart." He promised to cover for me. It turned out all I needed was one day, a brilliantly blue Marin County day. I took a head-clearing, spirit-lifting hike to the top of Mount Tamalpais, the highest coastal mountain in California, and right in our backyard. I sat there for a while by myself and realized Mel was right: we'd feel defeated if we closed the catalogue. In the end, by contracting the business, we'd be constricting the upside and end up feeling even more trapped. We *couldn't* go backward. We had to leap. Mel's point was that if we could grow the company a little larger, we'd generate enough money to hire competent help to get organized. There was no other way out of our problem. I went back to work.

I knew Patricia didn't mean it when she said we had to shut down the catalogue. It was just a cry for help. What she meant was that things had to change. She was right. We'd been doing virtually everything on the fly, without ever really "knowing" how to do any of it except as we had taught ourselves. As easily as we fell in love with each other, we fell into business with each other. We wasted no more thought on partnering in business than we did on partnering in life. We were natural soul mates, and from the start, we knew it. But we were reaching a place where what had worked for us in getting into business was now beginning to work against us. As much as we were empowered by and loved the idea of being professional amateurs, it was wearing us ragged.

As I saw it, Banana Republic was a product of us. It could not go down. It could *only* expand, never contract. Making business was not a problem, running it was. We didn't have enough competent help. We needed better employees who had experience in mail order and retail. But smart and talented people did not work at the wages we could pay. Where to get the money—and yet stay free of obligations to anyone but ourselves?

Closing the catalogue was unthinkable. It held the key to our future. The store brought us to Mill Valley, but the catalogue took us to the world. Furthermore, as difficult as it was to keep going, the catalogue was our surest moneymaker.

Here was my plan: create the best catalogue yet, add another color, and quintuple the quantity we mailed to nearly a million. We would need to rent a lot of lists. I'd been testing most of these in smaller mailings, and I knew which lists could yield the best results. We had to draw out customers on a wider scale. Assuming that the response held close to what we had been getting on the smaller test mailings—now 6 percent, more than three times the average in the catalogue business—we would generate enough cash to open a second store. The second store, as a third profit center, would justify the cost of the warehouse and the extra level of management.

Granted, it was a loopy path: mail more copies of the catalogue to generate the money to open a second store that would scale us up just enough to hire the people we needed to keep the catalogue open. But it was a plan we could finance ourselves. Our only out-of-pocket expense would be the extra postage. The list-rental agencies, the printer, and the suppliers were by now all agreeable to "terms." Only the U.S. Post Office required cash on the spot.

The plan worked. In less than two months, we generated the money necessary to open a second store in San Francisco, a half hour away over the Golden Gate Bridge. I felt certain that we would do three times the business there that we had been doing in Mill Valley.

We used our newfound logic to select a store location, pinpointing the San Francisco zip codes with the highest response to our catalogue. As we guessed, they were Russian Hill and Pacific Heights. A commercial section of Polk Street with a neighborhood feel sat in a valley between both. The rents there were reasonable. Serendipitously, a storefront opened on what we felt would be one of the best possible blocks. It was in a small building: twelve hundred square feet of retail space on the ground floor with a rented apartment upstairs. Unlike highly regulated Mill Valley, there was no design review board. To compensate for the subprime location, we painted bold black zebra stripes across both stories of the twenty-foot-high white building. Passersby could not ignore it.

In a welcome contrast to the dark, cramped Mill Valley store, the space was a big, empty white box, a blank canvas fifteen feet wide by eighty feet deep, with twelve-foot ceilings and two large display windows on both sides of the entrance door. After sketching several options, I settled on using the front windows to reproduce an inhabited scene similar to the ones I'd been drawing for the catalogue covers: an old typewriter, binoculars, and a few books on Africa cluttering an old, weathered rolltop desk, with a safari jacket hung over the back of the chair.

For the interior of the store, I sketched an exotic environment we could fabricate economically. Palm trees grew out of chicken wire and fabric. Papier-mâché begat colorful parrots. We painted a blue sky with clouds on the high ceiling and hung a camouflage net filled with palm fronds and leaves, simulating a forest canopy. In the middle of the store, we painted the floor with a resin-coated creek, and built a bridge over it to transport customers out of the jungle and into an Astroturf meadow with leopard print dressing rooms in the far back.

A smiling young woman, sparkling with charm, walked in the door.

"Are you looking for help?" she asked.

"Well, actually," I answered, looking her over, "we've been looking for someone just like you." (Intuition isn't infallible, but on the other hand, logical thinking isn't all it's trumped up to be.) Randi Hoffman turned out to be the best salesperson, then manager, that we ever found.

The city store was bigger, lighter, and, from day one, way more profitable. We supplemented the surplus with some new merchandise found at trade shows that fit the concept: tropical-weight wool trousers, cotton safari jackets, T-shirts, and fatigue pants, all new and in a full range of sizes. As Mel predicted, our sales were double and soon triple Mill Valley's. As Mel had also planned, the new money went back into the catalogue. The response from the next catalogue was better than we hoped for. He had a knack for picking and testing the mailing lists, and I had discovered a certain thrill in analyzing the pages by the square inch, selecting what to put where, predicting within a few units how many of any item would sell in each space. Sales were now booming, and we finally began to hire more experienced employees.

Solving one problem, however, now created yet another: we had picked the domestic surplus stockpiles clean of anything worthwhile. Although we filled some gaps with the new merchandise from wholesalers, the company's appeal was built on exotic surplus finds, and our survival depended on the generous margins the surplus allowed. We couldn't keep diluting our brand with items otherwise easily available, or cutting our margins with expensive wholesale products such as quality khaki pants and sweaters newly manufactured by other companies but with our labels sewn in. Sooner rather than later, we would need to figure out how to produce our own original line. In the meantime, we needed an urgent solution. We had a roaring business . . . with a dwindling supply. Fortunately, Mel was already on it.

14

Her Majesty's Leftovers

The answer was Europe, with its feast of distinctly different countries, each with an army of its own and its own cache of surplus. The reporter in me did a little snooping, made some phone calls. I learned that the man to see was Cobles in London.

I scribbled down the address and handed it to the taxi driver. He winced, then looked up at us shaking his head.

"You sure this is where you want me to take you?"

"Why?" I asked.

"Why?" He offered no explanation beyond repeating my question. Just shrugged, turned around, and started driving.

Patricia and I exchanged a quizzical look. You could not expect a surplus dealer to set up shop in a posh London district like Mayfair. Conceit of youthful abandon kept us from probing further.

We crossed the Thames. As we drove deeper into the East End, we watched the streets lose their polish and turn more raw. Twenty minutes later, the taxi stopped in front of a decaying four-story building spanning half the block. After we paid him, the driver sped away.

No sign, only a small door with the number on it. I knocked. An eye filled the peephole. We could hear locks slide. The door opened, and a short, grizzled man with crumbling posture and vacant eyes took a step back from the doorway, pointing his thumb over his shoulder to the long hallway behind him, at the end of which was a glass-walled office. Only our footsteps broke the silence.

I had called the week before from California. We were expected. Nonetheless, the suddenness of the heavy door clanking shut behind us played to the taxi driver's disturbing demeanor. I walked behind Patricia with my hand on the back of her waist. Two large figures in the glass office at the end of the hall stood as they saw us approach. Obviously father and son, both of generous girth. To our great relief, their eyes twinkled, and they smiled warmly. Cobles Senior, with a distinguished mane of white hair, dressed in a three-piece black suit and ascot, tottered from behind his imposing wooden desk, followed by Junior, same apple cheeks but with curly dark brown hair, dressed in a crisp white polo shirt and khakis.

"The Zieglers from sunny California, I presume," said Senior, setting off a flurry of handshaking among the four of us. "Leslie here, and my son, Lawrence."

We exchanged pleasantries, and the courtly old man, his heavy frame making colossal demands on a silver-headed cane, led us into a cramped and disheveled adjoining room—"our showroom"—where mounds of jackets, sweaters, blankets, bags, pants, and shirts covered tables and a dozen or so chairs. Along the wall, dowels sagged with the weight of weary wire hangers that held other khaki and olive drab garments detailed with an abundance of epaulets, bellowed pockets, snaps, and emblems.

We had come to the right place.

Patricia began sorting through the "sample" piles. I joined the hunt, feeling as if I were Edmond Dantès discovering the secret buried treasure on the isle of Monte Cristo. I could hear Patricia's thoughts: *If they have quantities, our problems are over!* We casually set aside a number of items.

"What kind of quantities do you have?" I asked flatly, pointing at our sample pile.

"Quantities?" repeated Senior, beaming. His answer was to push open huge double doors and usher us through the threshold with his cane. The familiar dense, musty odor invaded our nostrils. Mountains of khaki stacked to the ceiling and spanning half a city block.

I stole a glance at Patricia. She was doing a monumental job of suppressing her amazement.

If there was a Nirvana of Surplus, we had found it. Sack upon sack, bale upon bale, box upon box, some covered with tarps and others bearing cryptic stenciled descriptions of their contents to which we had grown accustomed: TROUSER

LINERS MANF 1951 SIZE 7 QTY 48 VAR R/PKD 10-MAY-43, IT 508K COLOR: ORANGE QTY 24 EA KEEP DRY HANDLE WITH CARE, CP 8405-99 CREWS No. 6 OLD PATTERN SIZE 12 QTY 4, DRAWERS WOOLEN SHORT, SIZE 3, FALKLANDS, SWIM TRUNK 50 EA COLOR: STRP B/W.

We stopped at an eight-foot-high pile of navy melton wool short-waisted civil defense jackets from World War II, knowing we could sell every single one of them. Customers would have snatched copies of these jackets for hundreds of dollars in high-end boutiques. And there was just about everything else imaginable: olive drab long johns, more Ghurka shorts (even in sizes other than 32!), pleated khaki trousers, thermal shirts, leather-bound berets, linen horse feed bags, gloves, socks, boots, belts.

"Nice selection," slipped from my lips. Patricia pinched me.

"We are purveyors of the finest tailored garments from Her Majesty's Royal Navy, Army, and Air Force, and the British Empire, such as it was," Mr. Cobles Senior stated in his broad British accent.

There was pride in the man. And an ever-growing, wily twinkle in his eye.

"I can't believe all this still exists!" I whispered excitedly to Mel when we were out of earshot behind a pile of British Navy greatcoats. "Do you know what you would have to pay for fabric like this today? Feel this melton wool greatcoat. Some of these jackets look like they were made on Savile Row. And in the original bales, still unused! I'm afraid to hear his prices."

"Doesn't matter," Mel whispered back.

I nodded.

"Right, then!" Cobles Junior said as we came back into view. "Shall we trot on up to the next floor?"

We looked at each other. Lawrence caught it and smiled.

"Think you were done for the day, did you? There's three more floors and another building as well."

The Cobles were gentlemen and treated us like visiting dignitaries. They were upbeat and genuinely pleasant. In dealing with Zimm, we had learned it was important to haggle but also important to give him something close to his price. We approached the Cobles the same way. That made things easy. To our amazement, the prices were as good or better than what we'd been paying in the States for U.S. surplus.

Terms?

Sixty days to pay *after* the goods cleared U.S. customs, Senior offered, no questions asked. They would arrange for a container, and "the goods will be on the water by the end of the week."

The Cobles had a car waiting to take us back to our hotel.

"Can we get you some tickets?" young Cobles offered, poking his head into the window of the car. "Any shows you'd like to see?"

Andrew Lloyd Webber's *Cats* had just opened in the West End. We had tried to get tickets, but the show had been sold out for months in advance.

That night we found ourselves sitting in row D, center.

A few years later on another trip to London, now by far his best customers, we reminisced with Cobles Senior about this first visit.

Mel asked him, "How much of the stuff we bought from you that day did you think we would never sell?"

"You want me to be perfectly factual with you?" he asked.

"Always."

"Ninety percent of it!"

15

Now, *There's* an Idea

With the largesse from Cobles, we were back in business with plenty of new merchandise. The quality of the British surplus was better and more novel, leading to more sales. Enough money came through the mail and the stores to hire Dennis Colbert, who had worked in operations at the Sharper Image, another catalogue company in San Francisco, to supervise getting the orders processed and out the door efficiently.

We also bought a computer, an IBM PC, which made

our lives a lot easier once we figured out what to do next after the mystifying little yellow C > flashed on the black screen. I was thrilled that we could manage our mailing list on it and found a typist to enter the tens of thousands of names of buyers and catalogue requesters that we had been storing on individual IBM computer cards. Ever since we mailed the first catalogue, I had been tormented by nightmares in which the trays storing these cards somehow got stolen or destroyed and having to start Banana Republic all over again.

By 1981, we had outgrown the full-moon-flooding warehouse in Sausalito and moved to 410 Townsend Street in the South of Market area of San Francisco, a building that has since won fame as breeding offices for web start-ups that go on to the big time. We hired a few phone order takers, a truck driver, some people to pack the orders, a bookkeeper, and a few other employees. Best of all, Patricia hired Kevin Sarky, a recent graduate of the San Francisco Academy of Art University, and trained him to render drawings that she herself had been doing of every item in the catalogue, freeing up a good chunk of her time.

We began to take a look at the next layer of problems we faced: sizing, for instance, and the perennial paucity of merchandise for women.

In the early days, when I worked in the Mill Valley store, our survival depended on selling what we had. Since the military consisted mostly of men, surplus didn't include much in the way of women's clothing. This made things more than a little tricky.

Most of the customers who came into the store were female. In the go-with-what-you-got spirit, I relied on styling to adapt many of the men's garments for women. Men's shirts and some jackets were cinched at the waist with Gaucho or ammo belts. Fatigues were belted or worn lower slung on the hips with shrunken tank tops. Plus I had the prolific Anna, our sole seamstress, converting shirts into dresses and skirts as fast as we could sell them.

But as we grew, a rotating cast of salespeople replaced me selling in the stores, some better at styling than others. In the catalogue, styling was next to impossible. Our illustrated format precluded showing live models wearing the clothes. We were losing countless sales and a big opportunity with the women's market, which we now estimated to be about 60 percent of our customers. When women bought items for their boyfriends or husbands, as they did frequently, they always checked to see what we had in the Banana Republic style that they might wear. It was painful to disappoint them.

We were also losing a huge number of sales because we rarely had a full range of sizes. This was slightly less of a problem in the stores, where both men and women could try on different sizes and see what worked. But in the catalogue side of the business, it resulted in more and more returns, many with notes from frustrated customers indicating that they loved the item, but it just didn't fit.

I had a vision for women's romantic adventure clothing like the safari outfits Grace Kelly wore searching for gorillas in *Mogambo*, or Amelia Earhart wore on her airborne adventures. I was determined to find a way to design and manufacture these items ourselves. This new direction, of course, required time, money, and production expertise. The manufacturing side of the business pushed close to the limits of my professional

amateurhood. I'd heard too many cautionary tales about the pitfalls in the process, the sometimes unexpected horrors of customs, or an entire line of a garment fitting incorrectly because of a mistake in the specs. One story circulating was about a company that sent a sample of a particular garment to be copied at a factory in Hong Kong. Somewhere along the way, the sample acquired a cigarette burn, and the order of several thousand garments came back months later with identical cigarette burns. We did not have the reserves to withstand such potential disasters.

And there was one more reason to get into manufacturing, the one that had been disturbing me for quite some time: it would put behind us once and for all the issue of building a future on a nonrenewable resource. We began to envision the line and knew exactly what styles to make. We wanted to start producing it once we accumulated the necessary funds. Maybe it was time again to pay a visit to Fred back at the bank.

It was going to be tricky to do. While we could see ourselves soon generating enough cash to initiate some manufacturing, we still hadn't tamed the complicated mail-order logistics. Dennis faced the monumental task of digging us out of the labyrinth of mom-and-pop systems we had created in order to install more workable systems. The bigger we grew, the busier we became, the messier it got.

Every day was another challenge. The stores were busy all of the time. Due to the ceaseless flood of orders generated by the catalogue, we had to ration the merchandise we sent the stores. A truck driver made the rounds between the Mill Valley and Polk Street stores and our warehouse on Townsend Street. One place was always short of an item that we had at another place. Having the barest of inventory controls, we didn't have a clue that the truck driver was also delivering "free" merchandise to his friends until he'd made off with more than a $100,000 worth of it. We needed better systems, better inventory control, better supervision in the warehouse. Dennis was good, but he needed help.

And other than newly hired Kevin, Mel and I still constituted the total creative department. Each catalogue had to have its own theme, every new item needed to be drawn, and there was the copy to write. That was just the start. Then came the typesetting, proofreading, tweaking color separations, attending the press check at the printer, renting lists—all of which we managed to get done while hiring, firing, and supervising everybody and double-checking to see that more bills weren't paid twice, more orders weren't shipped to the wrong address, more leather jackets weren't being stolen. On top of that, the two of us were the buyers, the merchandisers, the accountants, the sales trainers, and the go-to people for whatever was going wrong somewhere in the business at that particular moment.

Mel liked to say, "Where else can a liberal arts education be put to such good use?"

Meantime, the phone never stopped ringing, with customers and developers begging us to put a Banana Republic in their town, journalists writing yet another article on the company, retailers who wanted to carry our line, department stores offering to give us stores within their stores. It was madness, but a good madness.

We were becoming visible. In the retail business, that's an invitation for others to copy. Designers were coming to the stores and scooping up one of everything. For what? Ideas? To ship to Hong Kong and have copied? Several customers told us that they'd been to our store in Mexico City, and it was horrible how we chained the live parrots to the wall. And still others complained about cotton pants, bought at our Laguna Beach store, that fell apart after one washing. Mexico City? Laguna Beach? No time even to call a lawyer.

One of our favorite customers, Merritt Sher, a self-described maven of retail, a developer of shopping centers, found us very early on in Mill Valley. Every time he came to the store, he would banter for a few minutes and then say, "I want your store in my shopping center."

A tall, thin, puckish man with wiry gray hair, he always had a wildly mischievous glint in his eye. Because Merritt was so likable, it was my habit to laugh and say "Can't right now," just to be polite. But, in truth, I also had doubts about the shopping center he wanted to put us in, which was in a transitional Oakland neighborhood where I didn't think we'd do as well.

One day Merritt took the game to the next step.

"I'll pay to build the store for you."

I smiled.

"I'll give you six months' free rent."

Good as that sounded, the location was a problem, and I didn't want to be tempted. I decided to put an end to it.

"Merritt," I said, "we'd love to do something with you someday. But Oakland's not for us, not at this time. We can't even find enough merchandise for the business we already have. What we really need to do is concentrate on manufacturing our own line."

"Would you consider selling the company?"

Wow. Did he just say that? Never occurred to me. Who'd want to buy it? What we do is quirky; the business depends on us. But is he serious? We take his check, and he takes the headaches? Really?

I found myself thinking *Ibiza*. Never been there, but I liked the sound of it. I'd write novels, Patricia would paint. Lots of sexy people. Plenty of beaches and sangria. No worry about money again.

I raised my eyebrows and smiled.

"If you're thinking of selling, you need to talk to Don Fisher," Merritt said.

"Who's he?" I asked.

"He owns The Gap," Merritt said. "I'll give him a call."

16

Khaki, the Denim of the Eighties

A few days later in the Polk Street store, Don Fisher, tall, balding, highly alert, in his late fifties, shook our hands. With him was Merritt, as well as Maury Gregg, his CFO, and Sam Gerson, his president. After a few words, they all strolled in different directions around the store. Don absorbed every inch of space as if he were a video camera. He looked closely at the clothing, seemed to read every word on the hangtags, studied the walls in the dressing rooms that were papered with customer fan mail.

Grinning, he held up a ridiculous-looking pair of blue-and-white cotton ticking Official Royal Navy swim trunks that fastened with ties on one side.

"Do people actually wear these?" he asked Randi, our store manager.

"I haven't actually seen anyone brave enough to come out of the dressing room in them, but they are selling," Randi replied with easy confidence, adding, "They are only as ludicrous as the Falklands War for which they were issued. A piece of history for six dollars."

With the exception of Sam Gerson, we all went down the block to a restaurant called Henry Africa's: Don, Maury, Merritt, and Patricia and I.

Maury started by pumping us with questions. How often did we turn our merchandise?

"We haven't calculated it," I said, "but it seems like every month or six weeks."

Maury looked doubtful. "What are your gross margins?" he asked.

That one I knew.

"More than eighty percent."

"Oh, come on, you're lying," Maury said, attempting to be good-natured. "That can't be."

I shrugged.

"How do you plan your markdowns?"

"Markdowns?" Patricia took this one. "We don't mark anything down. If it doesn't sell, we mark it up."

Don smiled at her comment. I'd read a bit about him. A

bit of a scrappy start himself, although considerably better funded (old money San Francisco). He and his wife, Doris, opened The Gap's original store in 1969 on Ocean Avenue in San Francisco with the idea of selling blue jeans and records. The name came out of the tumult of the times. "Generation gap" was a widely bandied term to describe the chasm between disaffected youth and their parents and "the establishment." Don's inspiration for the store came from his own experience of having a difficult time finding jeans to fit his tall and lanky frame. The records went with the generation gap, a cleverly coded lure to attract the youth. To secure his supply of jeans, he made a deal with the Haas family, descendants who owned Levi's, also San Franciscans (*old* old money). Not long after opening his first few stores, he started selling private-label jeans and other private-label casual clothing to the youth market. By the time we met Don in late 1982, The Gap, today the world's largest specialty retailer, had grown to five hundred stores across the country.

I liked him. He spoke softly. He had a natural ease, a modest and unassuming manner, and seemed friendly. If he hadn't been wearing a sport jacket and tie, and had I met him randomly, I easily could have taken him for a farmer—probably a big farm, though. The total lack of affectation was notable. I wondered whether his whole presentation could be a disarming affectation. But the humility was genuine. So were the brains, I'd learn.

He was eager to share the story of how he'd licensed Ralph Lauren's western wear line a few years earlier. "Unfortunately, we blew it," he said, "because we got the sizing all wrong." It seemed odd that he was telling us about the failed partnership. He did so in great detail, in an avuncular style that made conversation with him easy. Nonetheless, my wariness would not go away.

Then came the questions, lobbed like court shots. What were our backgrounds? (Journalism and art.) Had we ever been in retail before? (No.) Where did we go to school? (Penn State undergraduate and Columbia University Graduate School of Journalism for me; University of California, Santa Barbara, for Patricia.) How had we financed the company so far? (Not easily.) Did we have kids? (Not yet.) More questions about the catalogue, the merchandise, the mailing lists, our sources, the concept, the customers.

"Khaki is the denim of the eighties," I blurted out at one point, not unaware that it was a tasty sound bite that a denim-of-the-sixties man could chew on.

He lit up. Maury gave me a skeptical glance.

"Your store is so creative," Don said, more animated now. "Do you think you'll be able to keep coming up with new ideas?"

Keep coming up with new ideas?

Of all the questions in all the world, there could not have been one more baffling to us than this one. Keep coming up with new ideas? Everybody doesn't?

"Ideas are not our problem," I said.

"What *is* your problem?"

Patricia told him we needed to manufacture our own line; we could no longer meet the demand with surplus alone; we needed a broader line of products to fill out our safari image.

Don sucked in every single thing we said. I could almost hear the information settle inside him. *Click. Clunk.* It was unnerving, but as someone who values the power of deep listening, I was also awed by it. The man was all ears. Of what use would he put the facts, tidbits, disclosures, and ruminations he was vacuuming out of us? We talked too much.

And then, abruptly, he asked, "How much do you want for the business?"

Now, *that* was a question, wasn't it? You'd think we would have talked about it or at least *thought* about it beforehand. We hadn't, probably because we didn't believe he'd be interested in buying us. A New York Stock Exchange firm buying a Left Coast renegade company irreverently named Banana Republic? Was life imitating art?

17

Falling into The Gap

I t does pay to go to business school, or at least to get all the professional help you can find, if you ever consider making a business deal with a man like Don Fisher. He made an offer. Not surprisingly, it was for more money than we even dreamed of, probably because we weren't dreaming of money.

Game changer. Amalgamated Gigantic Inc. wants to buy Mom and Pop Clothing Co. We needed a lawyer.

How does a writer go looking for an attorney? He

asks another writer, of course. In this case, his Spanish Paratrooper Shirt–clad novelist friend, Herbert Gold.

"Bernard Petrie," Herb Gold said without hesitation. "You
will love Bernard."

We *adored* Bernard. He embodied integrity, dignity, class—
yet he was playful at heart. *Purity* isn't a word you attach to
many people, but it exuded from Bernard Petrie, though his
modesty blinded him to this quality in himself.

The story here requires a brief digression: Patricia and I are
children of the 1960s. This tumultuous decade upended many
lives, particularly those of us who were in our teens and twenties.

All the news was bad: Vietnam; the assassinations of Martin
Luther King Jr. and the Kennedys; American cities burning in
race riots; police rioting at the 1968 Democratic Convention;
antiwar demonstrations and draft resistance—all of it for the
first time in history flickering on black-and-white television
screens in our own living rooms. There was revolution on
all fronts. In fashion, skirts shrank to mini. Bras were burned
along with draft cards. New music from the Beatles, the Rolling
Stones, Jimi Hendrix, and Bob Dylan challenged social norms.
Drugs were hailed as mind-opening, peace-inducing cultural
restoratives, with Yippies threatening to put LSD in city reservoirs. Students disrupted educational institutions in defiance of
their long-standing social and political values. These events and
others served as a powerful catalyst for a promising new "counterculture," social resistance on a massive scale symbolized by
flower children meeting guns, tanks, and police with flowers,
love, and hope. "Don't trust anyone over thirty" became the

mantra of a new generation determined to invent a future free of the underpinnings of corporate greed and the "military-industrial complex."

Going into the 1960s was not how you came out of it, particularly if you were a kid. For me and Patricia, on opposite coasts and still to meet, the social upheaval came in our high school and college years. It shattered any plans our parents had for us of living conventional lives. In our minds, our futures became all about freedom, the freedom to disengage from the safe and suffocating middle-class consumer-driven existence we each found empty. We were determined to live life our own way; the last thing either of us wanted was orthodoxy in any form, particularly in our work, and we saw self-sufficiency as key. In this regard, our families had pointed us in the right direction. Patricia's father worked three jobs and did all of the house and car maintenance himself. In high school, Patricia made her own clothes and worked in a department store after school and on weekends. My father worked twelve-hour days, six days a week, in his own wholesale business. I started taking odd jobs in high school, beginning with sweeping up a dress factory above one of the original Krispy Kreme doughnut shops in Scranton, Pennsylvania. With a newspaper route, other odd jobs, and money saved from working as a copyboy at the *Scranton Tribune*, I largely paid my own way through college.

I graduated from Columbia in 1968 after the seminal spring uprising when students, chanting "the whole world is watching," occupied several buildings on campus, including Low Library, where the encampment burrowed into university president Grayson Kirk's office. Not quite sure whether I was one of the rebels or a journalist—*New York* magazine was just then being resurrected by founding editor Clay Felker, and I had been assigned to write some articles for the new publication—I tried and succeeded in eluding the police and making my way into Kirk's office, hoping to report the story. (A few years ago, when I was cleaning out some old papers, I found a pile of Grayson Kirk's business cards, which I had lifted from his desk.) My report of the Columbia uprising ran in *The Miami Herald*, which recruited me as a reporter. Later the *Herald* assigned me to be a feature writer for its Sunday magazine, *Tropic*, until I was lured back to New York by a former professor, the late journalist/sportscaster Dick Schaap, who was then founding his own publishing company. A few nonfiction books followed, one with flamboyant New York congresswoman Bella Abzug. But ultimately the dysfunctional New York of the late 1960s and early 1970s, with its stinky garbage strikes and dogs unrestrained from leaving their droppings on city sidewalks, lost its appeal. I traveled to San Francisco to visit a high school friend on a sunny February morning and knew instantly I had found home. Next stop was the *San Francisco Chronicle*, where I became a sort of "Our Man in Nirvana," largely focusing on stories of the weird and wacky and wacked-out who gave the city its eccentric, free-spirited reputation. And then one day the most beautiful woman I'd ever seen walked into the city room, the new illustrator in the art department. Less than a year later the two of us walked out of there together to begin the adventure we now report.

Patricia, on the West Coast, was a little closer to the fault lines of the 1960s turmoil. She spent the Summer of Love as a high school student in San Francisco's Haight-Ashbury, dancing to the local bands: the Jefferson Airplane, Janis Joplin and Big Brother and the Holding Company, and the Grateful Dead. She didn't wear flowers in her hair, but for all practical purposes, Patricia became a hippie. The Vietnam War, boyfriends with draft notices, the Berkeley riots, the hypnotic solicitations of Harvard professor Timothy Leary to "turn on, tune in, and drop out"—everything was falling apart all around her. With UC Berkeley too close to home and in chaos, she elected to attend the Santa Barbara campus, which changed within two years from a Greek and surf party school to a hotbed of upheaval. The first year she tried to work within the system, gathering enough fellow war resisters to fill all of the ROTC classes, leaving no room for the pro-war students. But as the resistance movement grew, students rioted and burned a Bank of America building, the police grew more brutal, and she had enough. Off she went with a draft-resister boyfriend, hitchhiking and camping around the West, with a rekindled distaste for anything having to do with "the establishment." To sustain herself, she painted portraits for rent and food, and finally landed in the Santa Cruz mountain community of La Honda, living among poets, musicians, and counterculture Stanford professors. Her entrepreneurial prowess extended into making custom leather pants for rock musicians. After a year, she'd had enough of this, too, and decided to reengage, returning to attend the San Francisco Art Institute, earning her tuition working part-time at a market, where a customer, wife of the art director of the *Chronicle,* told her of a job opening that would soon lead her to me.

Through all these peregrinations, paramount to each of us was creating the free-spirited life we wanted to live. It was a future in which Patricia saw herself painting and I saw myself writing. We *never* saw ourselves in business—and that oddly enough includes even when we *were* in business. An artist and a writer on an adventure in the wilds of business, and that was it.

So here we were nearly five years later in business, but not *of* business, and the guy from The Gap wants to buy us.

It would have been a better idea to hire a strictly *in-business* attorney, not one who was even less *of business* than we were. I'm making no excuses for engaging Bernard Petrie as our lawyer. We became great friends and enjoyed many deep and fascinating discussions about his passions, which were constitutional law and history. He was an avid reader with universal interests, although business was not measurably among them. How could we have known? His father, whom we met and whom Bernard respected deeply, was as *in* business as you can get. Milton Petrie had been a Cleveland tailor who opened a dress shop that grew into a chain of 1,700 Petrie Stores. Well into his nineties when we met him, Milton Petrie could tell you, down to the dollar, what each of those stores tallied in sales yesterday. Bernard, his only son, lived like a monk and had no use for money. He quietly but resolutely asked his father to leave his fortune exclusively to charity so it would not become his problem to deal with. He owned no car, ate like a grasshopper, and lived in an apartment with only a single reading chair, a reading lamp, a table and chair, a bed, and boxes of books he was too busy reading to find time to buy bookcases for. As an upstanding father figure and friend, the best. As the lawyer representing us in a transaction with one of the savviest businessmen of the age . . .

At the time, we never gave a second thought to whether Bernard was the appropriate attorney to represent us. Why would we? Everything about him was to love. He looked like Ichabod Crane in Washington Irving's 1820 short story "The Legend of Sleepy Hollow": "tall, but exceedingly lank, with narrow shoulders, long arms and legs, hands that dangled a mile out of his sleeves, feet that might have served for shovels, and his whole frame most loosely hung together." His idiosyncrasies were winning: how he picked at and rearranged the food on his plate in restaurants without really eating it; how he avoided crossing bridges; how he could ruminate for years on buying a certain rug for his perennially unfurnished apartment, probably knowing all along he would never buy it. His one-man office on Battery Street was musty with yellowing papers spilling out of boxes, file cabinets everywhere, and a secretary who looked and sounded like a sixty-year-old Betty Boop.

"Mis-ter-Pee-Trees office," she chirped when she answered his phone. After taking a message, she hung up abruptly without a good-bye, not because of incivility but because everything necessary had been said.

Bernard did warn us. He said he'd never handled a case like ours. So what? we said.

Perhaps our dream of handing Don Fisher the keys and running off to Ibiza fogged our judgment. If we had somehow landed on the doorstep of financial independence, wasn't it mission accomplished, and time to go off to write and paint?

Bernard's counterpart at The Gap was the appropriately named Ted Tight, the general counsel. He played the polite, lawyerly, collegial part with Bernard while quietly smouldering with contempt for us. Why we irked Ted Tight as much as we did, if I had to guess, was our flagrant disregard for corporate decorum, and perhaps also the fact that two people, as corporately ill mannered as we, could be people who, by the numbers, Don Fisher valued more than him. For these or other reasons mysterious to us, the estimable Mr. Tight made certain that Don Fisher would be well advantaged and protected against the capriciousness of the upstarts with whom he presently seemed enamored.

The negotiations dragged on for four months, leaving us exhausted, and the company ignored and nearly paralyzed. And then . . .

Don called to say he decided he could not buy the company unless the two of us stayed on to run it.

"I wouldn't know how to run your company. It depends on your ideas and your creativity," he said. "I'll buy it, but only if you two stay with it."

"We aren't looking for jobs," I said.

"That's not the way to think about it," Don said. "It'll be just like you own it. Nothing will change. I'll give you as much money as you need to grow the business, as long as it's profitable. You'll get a percentage of the profits. You can do whatever you want."

"But *you* will own the company," I interjected, thinking *and since we are the company, doesn't that also mean he owns us?*

"You'll be operating autonomously. You'll have total creative control."

"Autonomous."

"Total creative control."

"As much money as you need."

"Whatever you want."

Before Merritt introduced us to Don, we were finally doing okay financially. However, after four months with Gap people crawling all over the place doing "due diligence" while I was fielding Don's almost daily additions of new clauses to the contract (no doubt with Ted's resourceful suggestions), each more clever than the last, the company was depleted of cash and energy. We were left with two stark choices:

1. Start the whole process over again with another investor—assuming we could find one *and* get him interested in a company that was by now almost broke and near broken, or

2. Sell the damn thing, sign the five-year contract he wanted, and take the money in dribbles as an "earn-out."

Oddly, I found myself thinking of how I could remove my name from the burglar alarm company so somebody at The Gap could be the one to meet the twenty-four-hour plate glass service at the store at three in the morning.

The fifty-page document detailing the terms of the sale and including a five-year employment contract was drawn up and presented by Ted Tight. Bernard found little wrong with it other than the occasional typo or legal phrasing.

"Don't worry," Patricia tried to soothe me. "We'll have fun. We'll have the money to make the company what we dreamed it could be; and we can see the world."

She wanted to do it. I didn't know. By a vote of one yes and one maybe, The Gap acquired Banana Republic Inc. on February 1, 1983.

18

A Line of Our Own

mouton
collar and
cuffs

horn
buttons

side
entry
pockets

leather
detailing

pants
zip off
at knees

ankle
tabs

inverted
pleat w/
buttons

Now that we had all the money we needed from Gap's* open checkbook, we had a lot of new merchandise to find and design. Patricia began sketching a line. I did some digging to see if any of the factories that made the original British surplus during the Second World War still existed.

*At around this time Gap pared the article preceding it.

Don remembered an expatriate San Franciscan who ran a small buying agency in London. Off we went with a suitcase full of surplus samples to meet Richard Walker. Richard put his staff to work researching where we could find other factories that had manufactured surplus items, and he drove us to one he knew about two and a half hours north that made leather and canvas covers for rifles. There we found Mr. Brady, the sexagenarian grandson of the founder, dressed in a tweed jacket and tie. He oversaw a few dozen gray-haired craftsmen on creaking benches, attending to their ancient sewing machines. They were finishing or repairing bags the factory was presently making for fishermen. Fishermen, such as there were, Mr. Brady informed us. The demand for fishermen's bags in England in the early 1980s had abated. Much of the business now was in repair, and there wasn't even much of that. True to their promise, the Brady bags that had been sold in prior decades had proven nearly indestructible. As a courtesy to owners of bags sold by his grandfather, his father, or himself, Mr. Brady repaired the occasional one where the leather or hardware failed. He showed us one such bag where the buffalo hide leather trim, cracking with age, was being detached and replaced. It belonged to Prince Philip.

While it was only the rare Brady customer who needed a new fishing bag, we saw that the bags could also be useful for multiple other purposes: to carry cameras, wallets, passports, papers—anything where a shoulder bag was helpful.

The order we placed was appreciated, and the deal was sealed with afternoon tea.

Over the week we traveled from one archaic, forgotten, out-of-the-way factory to another. It was gratifying to see that these outmoded yet authentic factories still existed and were oblivious to the frivolous whims of fashion. They used only pure fibers: cottons, linens, and wools, and created classic styles that functioned perfectly even in England's consistently wet weather.

At a trench coat factory in the Midlands, we watched craftsmen waterproofing the rubberized cotton coats with a process developed centuries ago by Jewish tailors called *schmierers*. Bent over sagging tables for hours, they hand taped and glued every seam, the *schmiering* process accomplished with their own fingers.

At another outerwear factory, we watched an antiquated process in which different blends of oils and waxes were added to cottons and linens to create jackets and coats designed to keep hunters and fishermen dry in the wettest conditions. Unlike the slick and shiny sweat-inducing plastic-coated nylon raincoats I had always known, these coats breathed. They looked like hand-me-downs from a British country lord.

A fur felt hat factory harked back to the Industrial Revolution. We ducked under a five-foot doorway, stepping down onto a packed-earth floor into a scene reminiscent of a Dickens novel. Steam hissed from hoods along the walls as grizzled elderly men shaved fur off rabbit pelts. Other men in leather aprons shaped mudlike mixtures of fur over hat forms. Upstairs, quieter, matronly women in thick spectacles sat pleating puggaree bands onto hats. Other women packed the finished hats into boxes.

We asked where the young people were. There was no work for them we were told. No one wore hats anymore. Mel and I smiled.

We visited an old mill that once made cotton ventilated fabric shirts for British soldiers serving in India, North Africa, and other tropical outposts. As the British Empire shrank, so did the mill's receipts. Here too our order was accepted gratefully. Elsewhere in the United Kingdom, a maker of leather military belts dating to the nineteenth century accepted our order and brought back retired craftsmen to make them for us. In Ireland, in low-slung thatched-roof whitewashed buildings on hills speckled with sheep and wildflowers, we visited factories making traditional Donegal tweed sweaters. We selected yarns from the bins of just-spun wool to be knitted into sweaters, vests, hats, and scarves that looked as cozy as bowls of oatmeal.

From one obsolete factory to another, we found respect for tradition unshakable. Sadly, however, the demand for their goods had fallen off dramatically because of the loss of business from the military. Oddly, no one in England seemed to even entertain the idea that the goods coming out of these factories might have appeal in the High Street shops. But we knew our customers' thirst for authenticity, and here, finally, were sources of unique items as carefully crafted as the surplus.

There was, however, a problem. These factories were rarely open to suggestions. When we wanted to tweak the fits, change buttons, make a small adjustment to the shape of a collar, our requests were often met with polite amusement, as if we were a couple of Yanks suggesting afternoon tea be served in Styrofoam cups.

Seeing our frustration, Richard suggested a small buying agency in Florence. He thought we might find more flexibility in Italy. One of us needed to get back to the office. I went on to Italy alone. Mel flew back to San Francisco to start on the next catalogue.

Florence was every bit as enchanting as I had imagined: an ancient, accessible city, with a nonchalant, well-worn beauty layered in history. Its language immersed me in a bath of warm childhood memories of spending time with my Italian-speaking grandmother.

I felt a natural rapport with Gerry Zaccagni. From the first moment he ushered me into his office, I could sense that he understood our aesthetic. We set out in his small Fiat to see a military bag manufacturer an hour or so out of Florence. For years, Mel and I had felt that luggage was missing in the line. In the early 1980s, travelers were still lugging around stiff, heavy suitcases or, at best, strapping them to little carts with wheels. We envisioned a line of authentic-looking carry-on luggage that was lightweight, flexible, made of natural fabrics, and every bit as sturdy as the Samsonite models of the day.

My notebooks held sketches of vintage military, mechanic, and doctor bags, and fin de siècle travel luggage. I had recently hired a bag designer to help bring the sketches to life. Niki Skelton turned the sketches into full-scale paper prototypes so that we could get a feeling for the volumes, closures, and distribution of weight on the handles. I now pulled the folded paper samples out of my bag along with my notebook of sketches to show Gianni, the foreman. He studied the paper shapes, then my sketches.

"*Va bene, ma . . .* " Gianni pulled out a pad of paper and drew his own sketch of the largest bag. "The corners, I think, need to be a bit stronger, no? Maybe . . ."

As if on cue, a man from the warehouse entered with a few pieces of buffalo hide. Gianni shaped one into the leather-reinforced corner he had just drawn. The small detail added a vintage sense of character as well as strength. This was going to be fun! I got an idea for the handle, which I drew onto his sketch. Gianni considered it, nodded his approval, then added a few stitch lines to my drawing. *Sì*, it was my turn to nod. He took another piece of the buffalo hide and shaped it into the tube for the handle, the end of which he gave a special leaf shape that increased its stitching surface, adding strength and beauty. So it went, back and forth, as we sketched together for nearly an hour.

In a matter of days, Gianni and his team transformed the sketches and paper prototypes into finished samples of a six-piece soft luggage line in pigment-dyed Belgian linen with a certified tear strength of 465 pounds per square inch, military brass zippers and supple oak-tanned buffalo hide handles, corners, and trim. Romantic, functional, roomy, and elegant—each one an object of beauty, an instant heirloom. I could not have been happier. England had its craftsmen, but Italy had artisans.

In the same collaborative way at other factories, sketches materialized into a knit traveling dress, linen sweaters, canvas and leather shoes, colorful scarves, and unique belts. Between design sessions were delicious meals with Gerry's family and side trips to the Uffizi Gallery and Palazzo Vecchio Museum, nearby on the Piazza della Signoria.

I would have loved to design the whole line in Italy, but due to customs duties and quotas, I was learning that it was more economical to manufacture certain classifications of clothing in different countries. We wanted to keep the prices reasonable. Fortunately, we already had a duty-free source for the leather jackets, Golden Bear, in San Francisco, where I developed styles with the owner's daughter, Shirley Winter, from patterns they had used to make jackets for the U.S. Air Force. Golden Bear was an Old World–style business. Each jacket was entirely cut by one expert craftsman and then stitched together by one expert seamstress.

For woven cotton shirts, pants, shorts, jackets, dresses, and skirts, Hong Kong proved the best place to manufacture. Unlike Italy, however, where product development could happen spontaneously in the office of the factory, Hong Kong needed a complete spec package and a sample garment. We set up a sample room in our offices with pattern makers, assistant designers, and seamstresses. It would take three or four production samples, sometimes more, to get an item right.

Henry James claimed that his novels each came from a tiny seed. That is how our line developed. All of Banana Republic's style was seeded in Mel's Burma jacket and the Spanish Paratrooper shirt. Consequently, the line was based on menswear. Even the dresses were shaped and lengthened versions of men's shirts. Men's shirts at the time consisted of either tailored dress shirts or T-shirts, with little else other than cowboy shirts in between. The detailing of the Spanish Paratrooper shirt and Mel's Burma jacket carried the authority of fine tailoring, while their weathered fabrics provided the nonchalance for everyday casual wear. This was the key to the line. Traditional tailoring, single-needle stitching, horn buttons, gussets, split waistbands—all the qualities you found in fine menswear (or for that matter, fine British surplus)—plus a few pockets, with the counterpoint of aged fabrics, for both men and women.

Because we were asking for a look they hadn't seen before, it was often a challenge to communicate what we expected from the factories. Our first production samples of a poplin "naturalist shirt" came back looking stiff and unnatural. Even with its tiny metal snaps substituting for buttons, the shirt lacked character. Well, Hong Kong can copy anything, right? So I took a shirt home, washed it in bleach, and left it crumpled overnight in a tub of strong tea. "Oh," said the staff in Hong Kong when they saw the distressed sample, "you like pigment dye and garment wash?" *Voilà*, the shirt could have been one that Papa himself wore racing with the bulls.

Inspiration struck in a cotton fleece factory the day before I was leaving Italy. Exhausted, I wanted to wrap myself in the luscious sweatshirt-weight fleece and take a nap. Instead, I sketched a jumpsuit with a drawstring waist and soft rugby buttons down the front, and asked the factory to rush a sample to my hotel before I left the next afternoon. I tested it curled up in my coach seat on the nine-hour flight back to San Francisco. As cozy and comfy as I'd hoped.

Well rested, I pulled on my boots and buckled on a wide leather belt as we descended into SFO. Mel was waiting in his car at the curb. His smile confirmed that we had a hit. He had a name for it: the All-Night Flightsuit.

19

Ask Not Why but Why Not?

Don Fisher kept his word. Except for monthly meetings—and the few times he dropped by the office, always calling first—we rarely heard from him. We started to assemble a staff. A bear to handle operations, Ed Strobin.

"Whatever you two think up, I'll make it happen," Ed pronounced, trading in his suit and tie for khakis on day one. And he did.

Suddenly finance and administration, poof! Ed made them disappear.

Our deal with Gap, which Don had spent countless hours structuring and restructuring with the wily Mr. Tight, was complicated. Simplified, we took a percentage of the gross margin, which meant that the more money we made for Banana Republic, the more money we would make for ourselves. The point was to grow Banana Republic fast and profitably, so Gap might get a little bit more value baked into its stock price, making Don Fisher and the rest of us richer.

Wall Street likes nothing better than exponential growth, and we were up to giving it a try. Our view was "Why not?" We figured that as long as we did not compromise who we were or diminish what Banana Republic represented, we'd go for the ride and see where it went.

With Gap picking up the tab—per the agreement to fund us as long as we were profitable—we decided to have some fun and open the next store at perhaps the snootiest mall in the country: the Stanford Shopping Center in Palo Alto. Because of the exclusivity it exercised in selecting tenants, Stanford was famous in the retail world for achieving the highest sales per square foot of any mall anywhere. Were we overreaching? Why not? I felt there were plenty of potential customers in the South Bay. If we could get into Stanford, we'd have no problem standing out—if only for counterpoint. It would be a kick to add a little grit to this self-consciously tasteful mall, where tiny gold-leaf signs on storefronts were preferred. Some high-end stores took understatement to a design level where it was difficult to discern their storefronts from mausoleums. We heard that the hopelessly bourgeois Gap had been turned down as a tenant. If we got in, we'd be in the company of Neiman Marcus, Louis Vuitton, Tiffany & Co., Bloomingdale's, and Nordstrom.

When Mel called the Stanford Shopping Center, he was told that no spaces were available. There was a backlog of merchants in line for spaces as they opened up. But Mel never took no as an absolute, only an inconvenience. He hung on the phone and kept asking questions. He found out that a small, one-thousand-square-foot space was just becoming available, although there were several offers on it already. Before he hung up, he arranged a meeting so that we could make a design presentation to show the kind of store we'd build if we were awarded the space. A copy of the regulations arrived in the mail the next day. Twelve pages of "no's" with the words *tasteful, existing, standards,* and *consistent* embedded throughout:

Storefront character to be derived from existing shopping center's vocabulary.

Storefront colors must be in good taste and be consistent with neighboring merchants.

Storefront materials must be consistent with mall's standards.

All awnings must be of standard Sunbrella canvas, uniform in shape, in approved palette.

No neon or illuminated signs.

"What? This is ridiculous!" I complained to Mel.

"Forget you ever saw it," he said, reminding me why I was so crazy in love with him. "Design whatever you want. If they don't like it, we don't want to be there."

So I held nothing back. I drew a color sketch of a storefront exterior with a World War II jeep protruding through the front window. Two living palm trees growing up through a rusted corrugated roof overhang framed the storefront. A life-size giraffe poked its head through the roof. On the face of the tin awning, the Banana Republic logo glowed in red neon lights. Weathered wood panel walls lined the interior. Hats hung along the rafters above racks and crates of khaki clothing. An arch of two curving ten-foot-high faux elephant tusks served as the threshold to the store.

We brought an architect to the meeting, Ron Nunn. He cut apart my drawing with an X-Acto knife, separating the foreground, middle, and background with foam core board for a 3-D effect, and mounted it inside a deep Plexiglas box frame.

Rosemary McAndrews, the design dictator of the Stanford Shopping Center, greeted us in a cordial but unceremonious manner.

"Show me what you've got," she said immediately.

Ron pulled the framed drawing out of his bag and set it in front of her. Her back straightened. We could all hear ourselves breathing. Her elbow resting on the table, she cupped her chin. In slow motion, the elbow came off the table. She leaned back, turning to face Mel and me, looking us one at a time in the eye, then said,

"*I LOVE IT.*"

I wonder if she heard our unified out breath.

"*I ABSOLUTELY LOVE IT!*"

Her ardor and the fact that she didn't ask for *any changes whatsoever* startled Ron and me, but Mel was more philosophical.

"What was she going to do? Ask us to move the jeep a few feet or make the giraffe a little shorter?" he said.

Breaking form creates new context, Mel believes. When context is unfamiliar, the lack of orientation gives people a chance to see something fresh.

Our plans specified stressed wood siding, aged corrugated metal, live desert palm trees, and an old Willys jeep. For the jeep, we sent an employee to the Southern California desert, where he located one: "still drivable, needs work, has original paint, 237,000 miles." He managed to drive it, sputtering, back to Palo Alto, where we had the engine removed before mounting it on boulders. It looked as if it were climbing over the rocks through the window, its lit headlights still beaming and its backseat loaded with vintage suitcases, books, binoculars, and a pith helmet.

"Looks like we'd better corner the market on World War Two jeeps," Mel said.

The store was a hit the moment it opened. On weekends, lines formed out the door. An employee heard folksinging legend Joan Baez say she would "come back when it was more peaceful." Malls tally sales per square foot as the measure of a store's success. Rents are not fixed but are based on a percentage of the sales, with a stated minimum rent that the tenant is expected to exceed. Therefore, the higher a store's sales per square foot, the more desirable the tenant. In Stanford and other high-end malls, it was no surprise that stores such as Tiffany, selling tiny high-ticket items in a relatively small space, were king—at $500 or more per square foot in those days. Clothing stores were way down the list. But we opened at $1,000 per square foot and kept going up.

Soon afterward, it seemed that virtually every mall owner was calling, offering prime space, sometimes even free build-outs. We were still partial to street locations. We had no interest in stamping out chain stores.

Mel and I agreed that Los Angeles seemed the likely next location for a store. Serendipitously, Don called one afternoon, asking if we'd fly down with him to look at his Gap store in Beverly Hills. It wasn't doing as well as it should, he said.

The location was a retailer's dream: a three-thousand-square-foot prime corner space on Little Santa Monica Boulevard, one block off posh Rodeo Drive. Gap's store there was a nightmare, filled with a sea of chrome "rounders," circular racks jammed with cheap, poly, shiny, froufrou blouses in candy colors, and garishly decorated jeans. In that neighborhood?!

"How much do you think you could do here?" Don asked us.

"How much are you doing now?" I asked.

"About six hundred thousand dollars."

"Four or five times that," Mel said without hesitation. I agreed.

"Well, then it's yours if you want it," Don said.

He sent orders to his CEO to close the Beverly Hills Gap store and hand the keys to us. Buoyed by our reception in Palo Alto, we pushed the decision even further, Hollywood style. Another jeep, of course, plus a full wall diorama with a life-size fiberglass elephant charging through the wall. To fabricate it, we hired an expert crew that had built installations in various natural history museums. The shoe department was a Quonset hut of corrugated metal. The dressing rooms were across a bridge over a creek with real water. A mix of living and silk jungle plants and vines added a touch of rain forest. For a final oomph, we brought in an authentic bush plane. When the aircraft was delivered, it required the closure of Little Santa Monica Boulevard and full police escort. The plane was hung from a blue-and-cloud-painted ceiling.

Until this point in time, specialty stores had never been designed to be more than . . . stores. Having learned the value of entertainment to enhance retail, we were eager to incorporate elements of theater. Now that we had the funding, we escalated what had always been natural to us: pushing limits that were limits for reasons nobody could explain.

Opening day, a line around the block. To keep the lines orderly, the City of Beverly Hills provided us with crowd control stanchions with maroon velvet cordons like those set up on Oscar night. The staff was more than ready to take on the crowds. Many employees were out-of-work actors. All salespeople were dressed in khaki outfits with "Banana Republic Guide" stenciled on the back of their shirts. We stationed two "guides" in pith helmets on either side of the door to admit people as space became available.

As on the first day in our tiny Mill Valley store, the sound track featured Cole Porter. The first people who entered, a distinguished and attractive couple in their midforties, paused at the doorway, surveyed the interior, then waltzed together across the floor.

It didn't take long for the movie studios to discover us. They started buying sets of clothing for the multiple takes required in filming adventure movies. We opened a separate Studio Services Division, facilitating studio orders for everything they needed without having to strip the store's shelves bare. *Top Gun, Under*

Fire, *Romancing the Stone*, *Out of Africa*, and *Commando* were among the many movies made in Hollywood between 1983 and 1988 in which Banana Republic clothing was part of the costuming. Also, many actors and other celebrities occasionally shopped in the Beverly Hills store for their personal wardrobes, including Harrison Ford, Tom Selleck, Vincent Price, Sissy Spacek, Bob Dylan, Christie Brinkley, and Steven Spielberg, to name a few.

We had no more worries about supply. Ed assembled a logistics team that dealt with the containers of surplus flowing in every other week. My mother was now the surplus buyer. At the same time, the new design development department translated my sketches into samples, and a complete line of clothing and accessories was being produced in Britain, Italy, and Hong Kong.

Every garment went from sketch to flats, specs, and patterns, which were made in-house. From these, seamstresses produced the first samples, which were then closely studied on fit models. We modified and remodified the samples until we felt we had something good enough to send overseas for a first production sample. The process required a team of experienced production people who oversaw fabric selection and development, as well as choice of buttons, interfacing, and trims. When we got it all right, the production people located the factory best equipped to manufacture each particular garment. Then, when the factory samples came in, Mel and I and other employees wear tested them to make sure they felt right and held up to their promise.

To help produce the catalogue we put together an in-house creative department of artists and writers. Now that we had the funds, we switched to a four-color printing process, although we still published the catalogue on uncoated paper that muted its color, preserving a vintage feel. We also began to advertise, but in print only: newspapers and magazines. TV was mass market and did not seem appropriate. Our visibility increased the media attention, which in turn fueled more sales.

A few days after Beverly Hills opened to the numbers we predicted, Don called to congratulate us.

He had only one question:

"How fast can you open them?"

20

"Dr. and Mrs. Livingstone,
I Presume?"

A trip to Africa was long overdue, and with the safari line expanding by the day, it was time to test the clothes in the bush. On the way to Africa, we stopped for a day in London to prowl for inspiration in the British Museum and the Victoria and Albert Museum. As always, I traveled in a bush jacket, which I now wore with khakis and boots from the line. Patricia wore a safari jacket with a white twill skirt and boots, all production samples for the spring line. Except for the surplus, we were by now designing and manufacturing all the clothing sold in the catalogue and stores.

When we hopped into a taxi to go back to Heathrow Airport, the driver gave us an amused but approving look.

"Dr. and Mrs. Livingstone, I presume?"

It's nearly midnight when we land. I'm hooked from my first inhale of the musky earth and warm, thin, dry mile-high air. Dark men in olive drab shorts, khaki shirts, and sandals scurry around in the dimly lit Nairobi airport carrying luggage. A porter brings our bags to the curb, and, appearing out of nowhere in the moonless night, a man drives up in a huge, roofless Land Rover with a sign on the passenger side of the window that says "Ziegler." I wave him down. He hops out with the engine running and silently hands us some papers, which Mel signs and hands back. Then, still saying nothing, the man turns to walk away. One look inside the Land Rover, and we realize this is a far more complicated vehicle than anything we'd ever driven.

"Hey, wait!" Mel calls to the man, who had almost disappeared into the dark. "Come back and show us how to drive this thing."

Since the man speaks only Swahili, the best he can do is instruct us by pointing to the gearshifts and instruments with a series of elaborate hand signals. He then vanishes. After a few stalls and jerks, Mel gets adjusted to the gearing system, and we manage to make it into Nairobi to find the storied colonial New Stanley Hotel and catch a few hours' sleep before sunrise.

We breakfast in the New Stanley's outdoor Thorn Tree Café. It is to East Africa what Les Deux Magots is to Paris's Left Bank.

Over bracing Kenyan coffee, we scan the crowd of grizzled safari guides, starchy diplomatic attachés, mercenaries, political exiles from neighboring African nations in turmoil, Kenyan students home from British universities, photographers with lissome companions, gunrunners, and Coca-Cola salesmen. It's a lively scene: animated conversations, head swiveling, and the occasional eye contact with a mysterious stranger.

But wait a minute. Something is odd here. I'm looking from table to table, and what is everybody wearing? Cheaply made, misshapen, ill-conceived, impractical, shiny polyester safari clothes! These are supposed to be the *real* thing? Here we are on our first trip to Africa, the couple from California outfitting America in safari garb, excited to finally set our eyes on indigenous safari clothing made here in the safari capital of the world, and *this* is it? Where are the safari jackets that enabled Hemingway's stealth in the bush? The skirts and blouses that cooled Isak Dinesen, the Danish author of *Out of Africa*, as she watched over a scorching coffee plantation? There is not a single trace of any of them. From a sartorial standpoint, we have landed in Polyesterville!

So it is that we first learn that quality authentic cotton safari clothes are not made or sold in this fabled outpost at the edge of the great African bush, the launching site for countless safaris into the Serengeti and the Masai Mara. Only ersatz safari garb can be found in Nairobi. We in California are the default source for the best selection of the real thing. If Kenyans were Eskimos, it would be as if we had introduced them to caribou fur.

After breakfast, we are off in the Land Rover with maps and two five-gallon gas cans strapped to the rear fender, down Mombasa Road to the two-lane "highway" toward the Tanzanian border. Less than thirty kilometers out of Nairobi, still on the tarmac road, we spot on the distant horizon, small and faint, a giraffe roaming in the open, fenceless bush, nibbling on a treetop. Pulling off the road, we jump out with our cameras, closer and closer, giddily clicking away. Off the tarmac, now following maps on dirt roads, out of nowhere, a second giraffe—and all of a sudden, ten, twenty, thirty giraffes—lope across the open bush. Giraffes are everywhere, as they will be for the rest of the day. We had each exhausted a whole roll of film on the first one we saw.

There are no other cars, structures, or even fences to be seen. The vastness expands my lungs, my head, my heart. The road grows rougher, muddier. We follow some tire tracks until they disappear, driving across cracked rust-red earth where the map shows roads built by the British years ago. At scorching midday, with not even a shadow for a compass, we keep pushing on overland, over clay, sometimes through tall grasses, navigating now by wonder, oblivious to possible peril. Near some trees in the distance, large shapes move. Slowing down, we stop under a tree and turn off the engine, alone in the immense quiet under a brilliant African sky. Elephants, a small herd. We climb out, walk tree to tree, closer and closer, until we can hear their breathing and snorting. We smell them.

Here we are, just the two of us, the elephants, the bush, and the open sky. Their tusks, imposing; wrinkled, sagging skin; alert eyes; large, flapping ears. Babies crouch under mothers' bellies.

Our eyes follow them until they disappear on the horizon. Walking back to the Land Rover, we spot a massive Cape buffalo. He sees us too. As we click away on our cameras, he ferociously paws the ground. We scurry back to the Land Rover, and drive away. Quickly.

We have no idea where we are until we see the unmistakable profile of snowcapped Mount Kilimanjaro looming in the mist. On the cracked vermilion earth, I spot a perfectly preserved, sun-bleached wildebeest skull. Mel stops to take a photo of me holding it. The earth starts to tremble, a growing kettledrum roll from a dust cloud coming in our direction. We have wandered far from the Land Rover. We run to the shelter of the nearest thorn tree as the rumbling becomes deafening. Out of the dust, horns and hooves—hundreds, thousands—a thundering river of wildebeest streams past us. They keep coming, for at least ten minutes, galloping at breakneck speed, threatening our small margin of safety, mesmerizing us with their pure force.

When we resume driving, a lodge appears on the horizon before we know we need sleep.

The next day, on our last can of gas, we drive north for hours, disoriented in the tall grass and covered in fine red-clay dust. Finally we spot a tall lone Masai tribesman who, to our relief, points when we ask, "Nairobi?" On the way back, we see a group of Masai women, elegantly wrapped in bright layers, with their colorfully beaded jewelry. I'd never worn much jewelry; I don't even have a wedding ring. But the Masai jewelry enchants me. I want it for the catalogue.

As we walk through the hotel lobby, leaving dusty boot prints on the polished floor, Mel notices a headline in the Nairobi newspaper:

MAN KILLED BY CAPE BUFFALO

Okay, we weren't going to find quintessential safari clothes here, but there was no way we were leaving empty-handed. Back in Nairobi, we looked for someone to help us to connect with the Masai and found our way to a shop called African Heritage. It was filled with African art, crafts, jewelry, and also clothing made from native materials but in more Western styles. The owner was in the back. A wistful and distinguished-looking American expat named Alan Donovan appeared.

After a stint in the Peace Corps in Biafra and a few years working in Uganda during the insane Idi Amin era, a time of random extrajudicial killings and extreme repression, Alan had seen a horrific side of life on the continent. But he was too smitten to be shaken. Kenya became his home, and he became what Kenyans call "a white African." A trained jewelry designer, Alan became a collector of African art and now was cofounder with a partner (then the vice president of Kenya) of this stunning pan-African gallery. The gallery also served as a cafe and center of African culture in the capital. We became fast friends. He had connections to many local tribal leaders, owned a large jewelry manufacturing workshop, and was determined to raise the visibility of African culture worldwide. Alan showed us a wide range of large exotic jewelry that he had designed. Lovely as it was, Patricia could not take her eyes off a roughly carved set of a silver-leaf necklace, earrings, and cuff displayed in a case.

"They're exquisite," she said.

"Turkana tribe," Alan declared. "Traditional pieces. They melt down old aluminum pots and pans into clay molds and hand-carve designs into each piece as it cools. I have this set, and another if you like."

"Can you get us a thousand of them?" Patricia asked.

Alan grinned. His heart was in promoting indigenous crafts. He knew how much medicine, how many textbooks, an order of this size could bring the Turkana.

"I'll get it done," he promised. "I'll get them made. Somehow."

He bought up a truckload of new aluminum pots and pans and drove north to Turkana country to meet with a chief he knew. No way, the chief informed him. The Turkana would never use new pots and pans to make jewelry, only old ones found in the bush. Ever resourceful, Alan drove through village after village, offering his new pans in exchange for used ones.

Word spread, and women came running out of their houses with all their old pots. Filling gunnysacks with the many pots he collected, he chartered a small plane to fly over the Turkana region and drop them into the bush where the Turkana could find them. Two months later, we had our order.

Alan insisted we visit Peter Beard, already a noted photographer and author, before we left. Peter, a blond New Yorker now deeply tanned, welcomed us at his Hog Ranch wearing a turquoise-striped kikoi cloth wrapped sarong style. His tented camp, on a grassy knoll where giraffes came to feed and hedgehogs played, would today be called an art installation. There were four spacious weathered green canvas tents mounted on saplings: a studio tent, another for sleeping, a dining tent with tables and chairs, and a parlor tent with carpets and furnishings that looked as if they could have come from Karen Blixen's house. Photo vignettes of stately and beautiful tribal women in hand-drawn frames, animal vertebrae, dried plants, feathers, skulls, hand-carved tools, sketches, and notes decorated his walls. His illustrated diary lay open on a table in the parlor tent, to which guests could contribute.

We gave Peter a prototype of a photographer's bag we had been testing and asked if he would review it for the catalogue. He agreed. His review arrived a month later, extolling the virtues of the bag as an ideal home and birthplace for hedgehogs.

21

Raising a Republic

With Gap's funding came management that elegantly executed the mechanics of our expansion. Don asked us, and we agreed, to hire two of his three sons. They could not have been more different. The younger son, Bill, warm, open, and jovial, became vice president of stores. Bob, wry, intense, and sometimes gloomy, took on the post of vice president of merchandising. Dozens of spirited new employees implemented what only two years before we had done entirely by ourselves. This took the company to a whole new level. What we designed, decreed, and dreamed up, they made happen on a scale that grew by the day. By 1984, only a year after the acquisition, we'd outgrown our five-thousand-square-foot office and warehouse on Townsend Street. We moved a block away to Bluxome Street and renovated all four floors of a twenty-thousand-square-foot vintage 1908 brick warehouse.

The ground floor became the warehouse and the shipping department. The days of having to wear wader boots on high-tide full moons to pack orders became a distant memory. Now there was a receiving area with quality-control inspectors, neatly organized with floor-to-ceiling shelving, and long packing tables where a rising flood of orders got boxed and shipped expeditiously. The second floor filled with logistics managers, accountants, analysts, a human resource department, and others handling the increasingly complex administrative demands of the business. Here leases were negotiated, bills and salaries paid, trademarks defended, permits and taxes filed. Sharing the floor were employees in charge of renting mailing lists, coordinating catalogue mailings, processing orders, and populating a bank of phones that never stopped ringing with phone orders.

The third floor was devoted to stores and product development. Bill Fisher oversaw the growing number of stores we were opening. Each one required coordinating the hiring and training of a manager and crew of salespeople, setting up the displays and windows, stocking the shelves, and knocking unfinished construction items off the punch list. Often Bill himself could be found working all night alongside his staff to meet a scheduled opening. At the other end of the floor was the design and product development department. Here were rolls of fabric and cutting tables. Colin Woodford, the new menswear designer, worked with a busy contingent of assistant designers, pattern makers, seamstresses, and fit models to get prototype samples ready to be sent to the factories.

The top floor, with skylights, housed the creative and merchandising departments. Here Bob Fisher managed the merchandising, production, and inventory control departments, which seemed to grow desks overnight. The merchandisers selected styles from samples generated in the design department, and then determined the quantity of sizes and colors to order based on the recommendations of Helga Baughn's team of inventory analysts. Penny Hammond and Bob Haeger, who a few months prior had handled the whole department themselves, traveled the world to find factories and mills, negotiate prices, arrange deliveries, track quotas. They also fine-tuned the details, checking that the fabrics, dyes, zippers, and stitching met our standards. The department nearest to my office and Patricia's was the creative department: a growing sea of artists and writers who illustrated the clothing, and wrote, edited, and art directed the catalogue and ads.

We were hiring daily. *How had we handled all these tasks by ourselves only a few months ago?* I wondered more than once. My job, of course, was to oversee it all, which, oddly, at times I found harder to do than doing it all. Managing didn't come easily to me, probably because I had the youthful conceit of thinking myself unmanageable. Bluntness, little regard for consistency, and bursts of compulsiveness are not usually what define an exemplary manager. At least I saw my shortcomings and was conscious enough to exercise spotty restraint in better moments of self-awareness. Luckily, good employees are not dependent on good managers, and we had a lot of them, excited and proud to be part of what was regarded as an exceptional company.

Maybe everybody was happy because we didn't fixate on profits. Instead we were focused on being a company as good as we wanted to believe we were and claimed to be. This had many employees finding hidden reservoirs of energy and talent in themselves. More enterprise and productivity were the results, creating a self-fulfilling prophecy and—guess what else?—those profits we didn't fixate on!

Having at the start of the company not known any better, we regarded profits as the natural by-product rather than the goal of our process. Of course Gap—as could be said about any other large, publicly traded corporation—was not natively inclined to accept such a casual approach to profitability, but our numbers spoke for themselves. By late 1984, our stores were breaking $1,000 per square foot, more than double the national average, and our catalogue was mailed to more than a million and a half customers, with still better than double the average industry response. It was generally accepted throughout the apparel business that we were *the* retailer of the day. Consequently, Don, as promised, kept his corporate honchos at a comfortable distance.

One employee said that working for the company was "like being in the crew on a rocket ship that's being renovated in flight." Truth is, we were making it up as we went along. Making it up with the considerable help of outspoken customers and imaginative employees. There were customers who so connected to the Banana Republic concept that they (correctly) felt welcome to contribute to it. They sent us streams of sketches, ideas, photos, thoughts—even their own favorite garments for inspiration and possibly to copy. Employees were often wildly inventive. One thing I repeated to anyone who would listen was my belief that creativity is not the unique province of so-called creative people. Creativity is always here, you just have to use it. Being creative is no harder and takes no more energy than blocking your creativity with the idea that you are not creative. Look, listen, take risks, and *libérez l'imagination*. The employees eagerly took me up on this challenge, and began reinventing everything from what a gift box should look like (jeeps, rhinos, and so on), to what was played on the phones when a customer was on hold (jungle sounds and language tapes), to wrapping paper (yellowed copies of a newspaper called the *Banana Republican*).

Ed Strobin sent out a memo that began, "If you ran this company . . ." and received a slew of suggestions about everything from the way to properly fold shirts, to sewing spare buttons inside the garments. A former colleague from the *Chronicle* turned mystery novelist, Julie Smith, came on board as a writer-at-large and initiated an intercompany newsletter named *Communiqué*. Louisa Voisine in the Beverly Hills store turned the Studio Services Division into a thriving entity. Visual stylist Kim Nunn created manuals filled with photos of coordinated outfits and tips that tutored store staff members in the fine art of creating attractive displays. Media buyer Jayne Greenberg suggested an ad campaign that would run like a serial, telling the story of how we found surplus stockpiles.

I had not imagined it could ever be so good. A great organization makes the boss redundant. That's what ours did to us where we were weakest. Now with Ed masterfully in charge of the operations, Patricia and I turned most of our attention to our strengths: design, merchandising, and marketing, where we were most happily engaged.

We were immersed in "the way" of every detail: the way the stores should look, the way the catalogue should read, the way the clothes should fit, the way a store employee should help a customer—down to the smallest detail of a window display or the word chosen to describe the color of an item in the catalogue.

The question behind all questions was how large could we grow and still remain unique. Because the funds to expand were easily available, we needed to be careful not to grow mindlessly. The risk was clear: our mystique was rooted in our start as a catalogue and store where customers expected to find a unique experience and authentic merchandise. How many stores could we open before we ran the danger of being seen as another chain store? How many catalogues could circulate, and how often, before we were no longer mailing to customers who valued the thrill of discovering us themselves? How many people could our first customers—the early adopters—see walking around in khaki clothes before they no longer felt so special in theirs? All this weighed on us, yet on the other hand, what artist doesn't want his work to reach the widest audience? To our surprise and delight, though I never would have believed it possible, during this period of Mach-2 growth in the mid-1980s, the brand remained soulful and truer than ever.

We had a complicated relationship with fashion, dating to the start of the business. At heart, I was still the "first available" clothes guy, although now a rather well-dressed one. I often said we sold clothes "for people who have other things to think about than clothing," restraining myself from saying "*better* things to think about." I can't say I knew what those better things were. It was my privilege in these heady days to be young and judgmental and leave it to an aging memoirist to explain the liberties I took.

My attitude gave me license to take harmless inverse swipes at some of fashion's inanities; for example, reminding customers that our buttons *did* button to something, that our pockets could actually hold things, and that the flaps or zippers to nowhere that sometimes festooned fashionable clothing were absent from ours. Who was I kidding? All the while I was knocking fashion, fashion was knocking on our door. Over time I quieted down, allowing myself milder follies such as naming our knit shirt without a polo player emblem a "No Horse Shirt."

Here and now in the second decade of the twenty-first century, overstatement has assumed dreary familiarity, and this may sound like more of the same, but we honestly gave it our best shot to make the highest-quality garments we could, classic in styling and indestructible in construction. I often kidded that we, like Mr. Brady and his bags, were unwittingly planning our own obsolescence, making ourselves "redundant" by outfitting our customers in clothing so well made it would be unnecessary to ever replace it.

It seemed that many people in America related to our anti-fashion stance—even if antifashion itself was becoming quite fashionable. Mel's playful swipes were better received than not. Wearing classically styled clothing in low-key colors with no visible logos, which included most of the line, gave people the pride of being unique individuals rather than billboards for designers. The media loved the concept and the clothing. Journalists adopted the styles as their own. The clothing was appearing in editorials in fashion bibles such as *Vogue, Harper's Bazaar, Elle,* and *Glamour.* We were caught up in the euphoria of the updraft, coasting along.

To Bob Fisher, a Princeton graduate with a Stanford MBA, the data from the growing history afforded him a chance to regulate the design direction that had been to this point navigated largely by intuition. Bob felt strongly that intuition was too ethereal and risky for a business of our size. I understood his concerns but felt equally strongly that while the analysis was essential to determine quantities, size breakdowns, and distribution to the right locations, it should never presume to dictate the styles. In matters of design, data give you the rear view—only intuition can tell you what's up ahead. An item trending up in the data didn't show that it had reached its peak until after it began to fall. In the clothing business, with months between order and delivery, this lapse could be much too late.

At one point, we were selling many thousands of an Indian cotton shirt we called the Bombay Shirt. The logical next move was to offer it in more colors. However, Patricia not only decided against adding new colors but also insisted "that it was time" to remove the shirt from the line altogether.

"What?!" Bob Fisher responded abruptly. "Are you serious?"

Almost from his first day, Bob did not seem comfortable in the company. I suspected it might be because coming to work at Banana Republic was his father's idea for him, not his own. Except for a postcollege stint in consulting and working briefly at Bloomingdale's, most of Bob's professional life had been spent at various posts at Gap. Without ever saying so outright, he intimated to me that his strong-willed father's prescriptions for him were a force not easily ignored. In his early thirties, his great passion was fly-fishing. He grew boyishly excited whenever talking about it, but I never saw him excited about anything else. His intensity, punctuated by a droll sense of humor, kept him mostly distant. In tackling his job, he could be tough, prickly, and fixated on the downside of things, the latter a long-standing trait that had prompted his family to bestow on him the sobriquet of "Nego," for a tendency to pessimism.

"Killing this shirt makes no sense," he told Patricia. "We'll lose a ton of business, and why? Where's the benefit in removing an item you already know will sell?"

"Because the shirt's being knocked off all over the place," Patricia explained, listing, among others, Eddie Bauer, Casual Corner, The Limited, and Bebe. "With so many low-end, mass-market, cheaply made fashion imitations out there, our customers aren't going to continue buying it whether we change the colors or not. We'll be sitting on tens of thousands of them, and not only will they be making the wrong statement about our brand, but we'll have to mark them down drastically to get rid of them."

Wincing, Bob was not convinced. He kept arguing, which he did with increasing frequency with Patricia. This argument and the others in a similar vein were, of course, about more than the shirt. By now we were adding a few significant pennies per share to Gap earnings. Bob considered it his fiduciary, if not filial, duty to make sure that we continued to do so. In spite of the fact that month after month we were beating "plan"—corporate lingo for projected profits—he remained skittish, questioning the very basis on which we had operated all along. Patricia found his constant challenges draining. While she welcomed rational analysis where it was needed, when Bob crossed over into design, color, or style—territory where he demonstrated no instincts—she was annoyed. Smart as he was, and he was, Bob didn't know what he didn't know. Patricia knew the brand she created, knew what it wanted to be and what it didn't want to be. Taste, knowledge, and intuition guided her. She did not arrogantly deflect suggestions; she welcomed them from those she trusted understood the brand. Ultimately, it was she alone who was responsible if an item sold or it didn't, and from day one, she had made remarkably few mistakes. Letting data crush instinct, or Bob's other inclination—to democratize the design process—was, we both felt strongly, the surest way to becoming just another chain store.

"Our customers expect us to lead, not follow," Patricia said. "We need to stay fresh and innovative, and keeping this shirt in the line doesn't do it." Her mind was always six to twelve months in the future about these things. On average, it took six months to develop an item from sketch to delivered garment, and in the clothing business, six months could be an eternity.

I agreed with Patricia. It was important to retain our position as a leader. The last thing we needed to do was copy those who were copying us. We repeatedly heard stories of "designers" in our stores scooping up thousands of dollars of "samples" to copy. The Limited had created an entire concept store, Outback Red, to unabashedly mimic us down to the number and placement of pockets on a vest. Even Ralph Lauren was suddenly interested in safari. As a matter of principle, Patricia refused to design or carry any garment simply because it was popular—it had to fit into her larger scheme of what constituted a compelling and complete line. She and Bob were on different planets on such matters, but autonomy means autonomy, no matter whose son he was, so the Bombay Shirt got killed.

A few days later, we took off on a trip to South America that was to begin with a four-day hike along the Inca Trail to Machu Picchu in Peru. As I settled into my seat for the long flight, I opened one of several newspapers I had brought with me and found myself reading in the business section of one of them that Banana Republic was a "high-growth concept that could soon make a significant contribution to Gap's earnings," which gave me further context for Bob's skittishness. I figured correctly that the press notice had been prompted because we had just opened our biggest and most prominent store of all, on the corner of Lexington Avenue and Fifty-Ninth Street in New York, across from Bloomingdale's. What New York had until then viewed as another fringe California company was now suddenly on the map. With a store that was hard to miss across from what was then the most trendy and fashion-conscious department store in the world, Wall Street, too, was taking note.

I hoped that sooner or later Bob would see that if he would just stop arguing, he would leave us more time and energy to develop new merchandise directions that Mel and I were thinking about. One was a line of children's sizes named "The Next

Regime," with many of the best-selling styles such as cargo pants and bomber jackets. But before we began putting resources to work creating the children's line, we had to deal with a pressing issue at the other end of the sizing spectrum. Customers were bombarding us with requests to expand into XXXL and plus sizes. At first, I resisted. I did so, I must admit, because I worried that too many larger-than-Hemingway people seen in the clothing would overtake the brand's image. Expanding the range of sizes created inventory problems as well (too many SKUs, or stock-keeping units signifying size, style, and color of an item), so I made the case that our clothing probably fit more than 90 percent of the adult population that fell within women's sizes 2 to 16, and men's waist sizes 29 to 42. This of course meant it wasn't only large people whose needs we failed to meet. The petite, like myself, were ill served as well. In our California stores, the most frequent requests were for sizes 0 and XS.

However, as we opened more stores in the middle of the country, the requests for plus sizes grew into a roar that I could no longer ignore. Nearly fifty letters a week from extra-large-sized people pleaded (a verb I use here without exaggeration) for Banana Republic to make clothing that fit them too. Most of the pressure came from women. Organizations such as Big and Beautiful wrote letters arguing that we were discriminating against full-figured women. This stung, because discrimination was never my intention.

So I relented, hired a plus-size model, and had the pattern of our women's Classic White Shirt graded up to a size 20. However, as soon as we laid out the pattern on the fabric, one unforeseen problem became apparent: the larger pattern pieces required twice the yardage. Another problem was evident when the model tried on the blouse: it was out of proportion, unflattering, and the buttons gaped over her bust. Patterns are graded up and down from the median size, usually a size 8. This makes a size 16 proportionately wider and longer to fit taller, bigger-boned women of average weight. But plus-size women are not necessarily taller or bigger boned. Our model was wider in the bust and waist but not in the shoulders or even the hips. To compliment her shape, we needed to design a whole new shirt style, not just grade up our existing shirt. And it probably would mean finding a different fabric with stretch or more drape. I was willing to absorb the cost of the extra material, but designing a whole new line for large people? It wasn't one of my priorities. I was more interested in designing a Banana Republic home line with bedding, carpets, furniture, and decor based on global indigenous influences that would appeal to the cultured traveler's eye. Also, Mel had a number of other enticing ideas for how to expand the company beyond clothing.

Notwithstanding the understandable grousing of some large customers, without exception we were getting outsized positive feedback from all over the country; hundreds of letters from customers every week. Because someone had taken the trouble to write, each letter, whether it offered an idea, an observation, or a compliment, required a thoughtful answer. These were the days before the SEND button, when writing to someone required pen, paper, stamp, envelope, and finding a post office box to drop it in. A charming, witty friend, Christie Allair, worked with me to answer every letter. One correspondent sent a photo of herself wearing the Serengeti Skirt while riding a camel in Egypt; another, a photo of himself looking rakish in a bush hat in what appeared to be his backyard. Sometimes I was informed that a garment had to be lengthened, or shortened, or loosened, or tightened, or made in blue. A doctor in Namibia wrote that the only complaint she had about her Banana Republic wardrobe was that the Roman Sandals squeaked when she was trying to sneak up on elephants sabotaging the Bushman water wells. A woman from Nebraska wrote that she got married in the Sacred Valley of the Incas in the Essential Skirt. Occasionally the correspondent would invite Patricia and me to come by for dinner the next time we visited our store in their city. Very often letters rained exclamation points and kudos on a "terrific employee."

All this feedback got us thinking. We were connecting with our customers in a way that to me felt holistic and resonant with how we viewed the world. Customers were literate and sophisticated. They enjoyed style and loved to travel. Why not explore a wider footprint beyond clothing, although clothing would likely always be the core of the business? Start with books. Our customers were keen readers, readily apparent by their reaction to the literary tone of the catalogue. We would build travel bookstores, I decided.

I also saw launching a Banana Republic–sponsored travel magazine. Surely our customers would appreciate a new voice in a field overfilled with titles that, with the then exception of *National Geographic*, were largely destination oriented and prone to sanitized and saccharine prose. Our magazine would publish experience-oriented, honest, nontouristy journalism. The idea for the magazine was rooted in our Rio experience and how it changed our view of the world. It wasn't the food that changed us, or the shopping, or the postcard sights. Rather it was the way that Rio got under our skins, made us move to a new rhythm, come home with fresh eyes. John Steinbeck wrote, "We don't take a trip, a trip takes us." And once it changes us, it changes us forever. For immersion travelers, our quintessential customers, travel is the experience of losing yourself in a new place. The person who departs is never the person who returns. A Banana Republic travel magazine would coalesce a new community of immersion travelers.

When I mentioned these new directions to Don, he became excited.

"We could be like American Express," he said dreamily. I didn't quite see the connection but thought, *Why not?*

Don was soaking in everything we were doing. He particularly noticed how integrated the concept was, with clothing, catalogue, ads, and message synchronized in tone and look, serving to unify the mission of the business. He complimented the wholeness of the vision and saw how it helped us to stand apart from other specialty stores. Not surprising, since most of those stores designed their products with synthetic intuition borrowed from trend services and color consultants, and then sought validation in focus groups. Advertising and marketing for chain stores was usually an afterthought piled on top of the product, not something that came out of the ethos—if there even was a *there* there in the first place. Sterile and largely unimaginative chain stores were just then beginning to steamroll over locally run stores. Enter formulaic corporate-run retailing, exit locally owned and managed clothing stores and small department stores run by your neighbors.

Although one of the better formulas in its early days, Gap, well into its second decade, had lost its magic. Don's own skills were in negotiating shrewd leases. He left matters of design, merchandising, and marketing to others, and over the years, their ideas had grown uninspired. This, he reminded us frequently, is what excited him about Banana Republic.

"The creativity around here," he said, "is flying all over the place."

Within a few months of acquiring Banana Republic, Don got the idea that he needed to reinvigorate Gap by hiring a new CEO to bring sizzle back to the brand. He put the executive recruiters to work finding him someone who could do the job.

I personally continued to oversee marketing. Because word of mouth and customer loyalty were so strong, and because we continued to enjoy heaps of free publicity, I kept our advertising budget at a minimum and instead got the idea to ask some of our well-known customers to review the clothes for the catalogue. Without hesitation, most agreed enthusiastically.

The reviews were witty, often hilarious, and they garnered much attention. One author told us that he got more compliments on his review in the Banana Republic catalogue than on all his books. Uncannily, the reviewers got right into the spirit of the company:

Actor Alan Arkin on the Correspondent's Jacket: "[It] has given me, at last, an air of mystery. I can leave places early, and no one asks me where I'm going anymore. They're all sure that I have important planes to catch in half an hour for secret meetings in the jungle."

Author Anne Rice on the French Naval Cape: "When I took it out of the box, I knew it was mine. Any self-respecting vampire would adore it."

Novelist Cyra McFadden on the Safari Dress: "Because it's

all cotton, it wrinkles; but so do I. The difference is that the Safari Dress wrinkles gracefully."

Writer Anne Lamott on the Leather and Linen Traveling Boots: "[W]alked to a restaurant five miles away, confident I could con anyone, anywhere, into mistaking me for a person of the employable persuasion."

Writer/director Nora Ephron on the All-Night Flightsuit: "I have not yet had a chance to wear my All-Night Flightsuit on an all-night flight, but that's only because I haven't taken an all-night flight since I got it. What I *have* worn it for is cooking, sleeping, reading, walking here and there, taking the children to school, and, best of all, just lying around."

Author Paul Theroux on the Globetrotter Bags: "The great thing about these bags is that not only can you bring them on planes, but they fit in all railway compartments and can easily be lashed to a camel."

Journalist/TV Newsman Pierre Salinger on the Traveler's Sportcoat: "When I see a fellow American in Paris these days, I have the desire to hug and kiss him, congratulate him on his courage in crossing the Atlantic to this land of tigers and lions disguised as terrorists. Of course, when I meet this compatriot, I am wearing my Banana Republic Traveler's Sportcoat."

Herbert Gold on the Sierra Denim Shirt: "What better gear for searching out the secrets of eternity? How could Shakespeare or Tolstoy have written Allen Ginsberg's 'Howl' without running questing fingers past the heart, molded to ample pockets filled with spare pens and three-by-five cards, up to the throat protected from cruel judgments by pensive yet courageous blue denim?"

Cartoonist G. B. Trudeau on the Aviator's Jacket: "[I]f people want to mistake me for Sam Shepard, that's their problem."

Actor John Lithgow on the New Zealand Tramping Shirt: "Who would have thought wearing a coat would make the very air seem fresher?"

Author Martin Cruz Smith on the Australian Fur Felt Bush Hat: "You ask what I thought of your hat. I thought it was a beautiful hat, and I'm sorry my dog ate it . . . I will not stoop to the suggestion that women fought to stroke my brim, I leave that to your advertising agency. This is a tragic story after all."

Finally, the gonzo journalist Hunter S. Thompson reviewed the waxed cotton Portmanteau Jacket and characteristically claimed he had stuffed the pockets with cash and lent it to a friend off to Costa Rica.

Long before the cynical and disingenuous days of so-called product placements and celebrity endorsements, we were just having a good time. It wasn't about exploitation. It was light-hearted repartee elevating clothing to a starring role in our lives.

22

The Muse of Travel

For over eight years, the merchandise decisions came naturally and easily. Mel and I had endless ideas for pants, jackets, shirts, hats, belts, and dresses that felt and looked like they belonged in a line of safari clothing. Now, however, the decision to widen the focus from "safari" to "travel" made the designing trickier. Clearly, safari was rugged and slightly weathered khaki, pockets, bush jackets, wide brims, epaulets, leather trims, and boots. Old adventure movies, books on international military uniforms, and colonial Africa and India, as well as the well-documented exploits of Denys Finch Hatton, Kenyon and Maud Painter, Karen Blixen (pen name Isak Dinesen), Teddy Roosevelt, Ernest Hemingway, and other more obscure adventurers into early-twentieth-century Africa were all ready sources for inspiration.

The new travel focus, like safari, required that the clothing still be function driven, comfortable in changing climates, and sturdily made in the natural fabrics that were a signature of the brand. Now flexibility, particularly, was key. The clothing needed to adapt from casual day sightseeing, to a business meeting, to suitable wear for a fine restaurant in the evening, so a full travel wardrobe would fit into a carry-on suitcase.

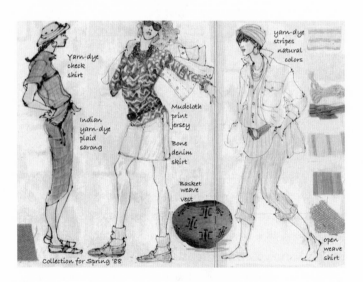

The new challenge was to instill in the travel clothing a sense of heritage that ensured it would remain as distinctive and authentic as the safari lineage. I snipped swatches from vintage pieces found in flea markets and old clothing stores, and sent them to the mills to duplicate the weave and hand of the fabric. Sometimes I sent the detail of a pocket or a buttonhole. The inspiration for a spring color might appear in the ochre of a book's page yellowing with age, the spark for a new silhouette of a long, romantic skirt, in a nineteenth-century novel.

What began to emerge was an international sensibility. In our travels, I was drawn to time-tested styles from remote cultures. The influence of sarongs, caftans, saris, *bombachas* (Argentine trousers), guayabera shirts, kilts, Thai jackets, and gaucho belts tweaked with contemporary fits moved seamlessly into the line. Indigenous patterns such as Malian mud cloth, batik, kente cloth, and Aboriginal dream paintings were printed onto tops and scarves. Navajo blanket and basket patterns were knitted into sweater vests. The jewelry that Alan Donovan was having made for us by tribes in Kenya complemented these styles perfectly.

By now we were traveling half the year in search of ideas and field-testing the clothing. Mel kept a journal of our travels, and I made sketches. We published these in the catalogues.

The changing themes of the catalogue, the clothes, and the store displays followed our peregrinations. We flew to every continent except Antarctica to find fabrics, styles, and details of authentic heritage, all the while learning firsthand the sartorial needs of travelers. Everywhere we went, we dug in and involved ourselves with the local culture. The journals, which became the catalogue themes, went from "Rambles and Scrambles Around the English Lakes" to "On the Road to Mandalay"; from "Into the Amazon" to "Soviet Safari." Mel's musings jumped from page to page throughout the catalogue, illustrated by my water-colors. To read the entire journal, a customer would leaf through the catalogue, discovering the latest merchandise along the way.

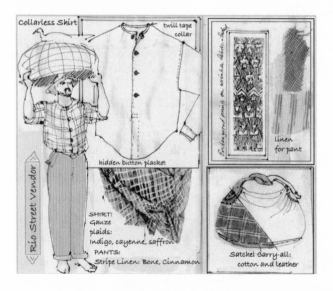

Random events during these travels sparked ideas that funneled back into the company, often in unexpected ways. Mel walked in on a maid changing the bed in a hotel in the south of France, and seeing the classic blue-and-white ticking on the mattress got the idea for a ticking shirt. Baskets of colorful spices in a Chiang Mai, Thailand, market enchanted their way into the fall palette. Mud cloths in Kenya morphed into a line of T-shirts and scarves. A market's striped awning on Lamu Island suggested a design for a sundress. Igor Stravinsky's image on a stamp prompted the idea to go to the Soviet Union in search of Russian military surplus.

My notebooks filled with watercolor sketches: the buckle on the belt of a man in the Rome train station, Burmese men and women in *lungis*, and Aboriginal graffiti on a bathroom wall in Alice Springs, Australia. Peasant bundles inspired the shape of a purse; a Johannesburg witch doctor's talisman, a necklace design. A Rio street vendor's baggy cropped pants and wide-cut collarless shirt influenced the styles for summer. An old, faded picture of a woman piloting a bush plane guided the design of our women's flight jacket. For color, smudges of ruddy Kenyan mud, salmon-colored outback earth, and rich Indian curry.

Experience was a muse. Pursuing our frisky African guide on horseback at breakneck speeds through the forests on Mount Kenya gave Patricia the idea for a long-skirted Equestrienne Suit. The voracious mosquitoes in the Amazon prompted the mosquito net T-shirt. Fig Tree Camp in Kenya spawned an idea for a store design.

Serendipity led the way. At a Paris flea market, we spotted an unusual Israeli paratrooper bag. That same night we were on a flight to Tel Aviv to find where it was made. Within a couple of months, it was in the catalogue.

In Soviet Leningrad, our new friend Danny Grossman at the U.S. Consulate shepherded us through a bohemian underground of artists and musicians and into the bugged apartments of whispering Jewish refuseniks eager to send out stories of persecution by the authorities. On the High Holy Day of Yom Kippur we stood with Danny in the cold night outside the city's only remaining synagogue, watching the worshippers file out, their faces eerily indistinguishable from the men and women in my grandfather's synagogue in Scranton, Pennsylvania.

Danny introduced us to the brilliant renegade artist Tolya Belkin, whom we commissioned to illustrate the cover for the Russian catalogue to be published upon our return. Our exploits did not go unnoticed by the KGB. Soon the television in our hotel room, which we had never even turned on, was being fixed by maintenance men at all hours, and we were being tailed by an ineptly surreptitious agent in a trench coat as if in a B spy movie. After being followed into restaurants and chased through the subway, we lost "Boris," as we derisively named him, by directing our taxi driver at the last minute to make a sharp turn onto an expressway exit and head to a different

Moscow airport, where we hopped on the next plane out. It happened to be going to Helsinki, Finland. Danny dispatched Tolya's unauthorized catalogue cover in the diplomatic pouch. We published it to much excitement.

In Florence, we stumbled onto an industrial uniform trade show and there got the idea that Italian cotton waiter's jackets would make elegant summer blazers. Patricia ordered a few thousand of them on the spot, to be dyed in ivory, khaki, and navy. The awed manufacturer asked, "How many restaurants do you own?" At the same show, Patricia found a cotton auto mechanic jumpsuit and ordered it in smaller sizes for women who were adventurous enough to wear Ferrari mechanic overalls.

In the Amazon, we camped on the jungle floor with a tribe of Indians who shared their monkey meat dinner with us and offered us the potent bark of a native tree to chew as a stimulant. They made Patricia an iridescent beetle necklace that became her hatband. In the Ecuadorian jungles, with a missionary's son as our guide, we took a dugout canoe down streams and tributaries filled with crocodiles, water snakes, even piranhas, to reach remote tribal lands in search of rarely seen indigenous designs. We slept for three restless nights in the jungle on a stilt veranda, wakened by rustlings, mosquitoes, howler monkeys, and the cries of other creatures of the night. The last night, with the rain slamming the palm leaf roof and falling in sheets over the sides of the veranda, we awoke at dawn. We'd both had the *same* dream about a snorting jaguar sniffing at our head. In Peru, we braved Shining Path terrorists, with each breath roaring in our ears in the oxygen-thin air of fourteen-thousand-foot passes, reaching Machu Picchu four days later. Climbing the neighboring peak, we caught an up-close glimpse of an Andean condor, its ten-foot wingspan momentarily blocking out the sun.

In Australia, we rode camels to Ayers Rock and made hot tea over an open fire to cool down in the 125-degree heat. Thirsty flies filled our ears, climbed into our noses, dove into our tea—and our open mouths. On the way home, we cooled off sloshing through four days in the wettest spot in the world, New Zealand's Milford Track. In Burma, traveling by dhow, rickshaw, and rickety Fokker planes with open back doors, I swapped my Casio watch for antique hand-carved marionettes. Patricia traded her dress for a sarong and an embroidered jacket. In Mandalay, it was safe to brush our teeth only with beer.

Weather was always a challenge, especially for carry-on travelers like us. One garment had to serve varying conditions.

During a trip to the Australian outback, chilly mornings gave way to scorching afternoons with nowhere to change, so I cut off our pants above the knee with my Swiss army knife, a mistake I deeply regretted when the mosquitoes came out after sundown. So came the idea for the Kenya Convertible pant, which zipped off or on at the knee. In countries that the British had once colonized, a tweed sport coat was a handy piece of clothing to have for its pockets, warmth, and easy panache. This led us to Savile Row to work with tailors on prototypes of a British wool sport coat. However, we found its construction too heavy; its stiff formality was not our brand. It began to show promise only when I tore out the carefully stitched-in horsehair interfacings, shoulder pads, and silk linings. Then we further softened the shoulders, bound the exposed interior seams, and added leather details and elbow pads, resulting in the classic-looking Traveler's Sportcoat that was as comfortable as a sweater. We sent it to Hong Kong to be manufactured in Donegal tweed wool.

And pockets, always pockets, a traveler's best friend. Appreciation of pockets started early. Mel was always jamming too many things into his: notebook, wallet, newspapers, keys, camera. I favored pockets over pocketbooks too, conscious of how shoulder bags disturb posture. When it was hot, we wanted pockets without sleeves, so we created a Mesh Portable Pockets Vest. Most popular was the Bush Vest, which we made in several colors of pigment-dyed cotton, and also a cognac-colored leather. Mel described it in the catalogue as "a walking desk with a drawer for everything." Our Photojournalist Vest, designed with the guidance of *Time* magazine photojournalist Matthew Naythons, became a staple for photographers the world over.

Whenever we passed through Paris, a must-stop was the flea market at Porte de Clignancourt—officially called *Les Puces de Saint-Ouen* but known to everyone as *Les Puces* (the Fleas). There we found a shirt of cool blue. The two patch pockets, cuffs, and collar were handstitched at the edges. It draped over my arm like fine silk. I checked the label: men's S, cotton and rayon, made in the U.S.A. Not natural, not French, but we bought it anyway. I wore it out to dinner that night with my Serengeti Skirt, feeling a bit of a traitor to my natural-fiber credo, but I was smitten.

"So make it in cotton," Mel said.

"Won't drape the same," I answered glumly.

"Well, what *is* rayon anyway?" and he looked it up.

Turns out, rayon is a seminatural fiber manufactured from cellulose. That was enough to ease my conscience. We reproduced the blend in Gauloise blue, aubergine, and cafe creme, and named it the French Cafe Shirt "in honor of the Francophiles of the past who sat for hours discussing Proust over *un café crème* on the Boulevard Saint-Michel." The painter Ed Ruscha reviewed it, enamored of the colors. "My shirt is a very nice shade of gray-blue, with even a little purple in it," he wrote.

The catalogues allowed us to share the excitement of all these travels and discoveries. They were whimsical mashups of merchandise, theater, adventure, and literature. Theater, particularly, was what we had in mind in designing and creating the set inside the stores that became the backdrop to display the clothing. The clothing itself, of course, had a costume quality about it—part of its attraction.

The catalogue was the road map for the business. It set the tone; it set the theme; it set the timing. Traveling as much as we did, except for my journals and Patricia's sketches, we entrusted the catalogue to the savvy journalist (now novelist) Meredith Maran, who, sizing up the job as "a big playground," brought it to a new level. She worked to seamlessly integrate the voice and vision of the business. Every piece of copy and every drawing was fussed with until it was perfectly "Banana Republic." By this point the company had established its own ethos and singular personality. I liked to put a glass or a pencil in the middle of the table at meetings and declare, "That's Banana Republic. It's our job to listen to it." I thoroughly enjoyed working with Meredith and others, including the elegant writer Nancy Friedman as editorial director, and Louise Kollenbaum as art director. Their playfulness and their fresh bright minds expanded Patricia's and my vision and made the catalogue better than ever.

Meredith wasn't kidding about the playground—she loved pushing up against its fences and lost no opportunity to do so, challenging the limits (digest size, all hand drawings, each item perfectly rendered in name, picture, and word) of the catalogue. No one in the creative department had ever worked a "real" job before. Every writer hired was a virgin to the world of business. Other than their writing, or doing odd jobs on the side to support their writing, until recruited by us they had never even imagined themselves working for a big "corporation," particularly in creative positions. They were fiercely independent, would not tolerate bullshit, and seized every chance they had, or could invent, to push things. In the latter regard, the puckish Meredith was the poster child. She sat me down one day and sternly lectured me about the name of the company. Was I aware that "banana republic" was "a disparaging imperialistic term"? I conceded that was one way to look at it. "But there isn't much I can do about it anymore except take Banana Republic off your paycheck," I told her, and we each had a good laugh.

The den mother to this pack of rascals was the talented Bonnie Dahan, who performed the impossible task of managing the creative department and keeping the playground safe.

From 1985 through early 1988 the catalogue grew exponentially, to a point where we mailed thirty million annually.

With the catalogue preceding them, stores opened in city after city every few weeks. In almost no time, we were at thirty-five stores, and by 1986, approaching sixty-five. We were signing new leases weekly, and projecting to have more than a hundred stores opened by the end of 1988. By definition, Banana Republic had become a "chain." However, that word, indeed the very idea of "chain store," grated on us—in fact, horrified us. So in spite of the number of stores we had grown to, we were determined to keep a chain store mentality out of the company. But how do you make a chain not a chain?

23

Size Matters

The first line of defense against creeping chain mentality was to be sure that no two stores looked alike. Chain stores replicate the same design in every mall, one of many economies of scale that help them keep their costs down and their profile ubiquitous. We, on the other hand, wanted every store to be a unique shopping experience that suited its locale. Also, because chain stores are synonymous with mall stores, we preferred to build our stores on vibrant shopping neighborhood streets rather than in malls. This, however, was not an idea that Don Fisher shared.

Don was becoming increasingly interested in the company, visiting every few days, calling with suggestions or questions, dropping in on Ed Strobin to take the pulse of the operations. When it came to siting stores, I learned, autonomy wasn't exactly autonomy. From his Gap headquarters in San Bruno, twenty minutes away, Don was now directly taking charge of selecting locations. I began to see he was using Banana Republic as a chip in negotiating with malls, leveraging us for better deals and better spaces for his Gap stores in the same shopping centers. I didn't mind. He knew the lay of the real estate business, was a master lease negotiator, and wanted to see us in top-end locations. Despite our preference for street locations, malls were where the business was in some cities, and Don knew exactly the malls where we'd do best. The leases started rolling in: South Coast Plaza in Orange County, the Galleria in Houston, Short Hills Mall in New Jersey, Water Tower Place in Chicago, Faneuil Hall Marketplace in Boston, Tysons Corner Center in Virginia.

While Don busied himself on the malls, I scouted street locations, and we opened stores as well on Newbury Street in Boston, Michigan Avenue in Chicago, Grant Avenue in San Francisco, Bleecker Street in New York, and Main Street in Westport, Connecticut.

Architect Russ Levikow was well up to the challenge of designing the stores, deriving inspiration for authentic elements and details from photos and sketches of our travels. The goal in designing our stores was to transport customers into the state of wonder and alertness that simulated the travel experience. They might enter under an arch of elephant tusks, the canopies of tented camps, or tin-roofed jungle shelters and emerge into museum-quality dioramas with trees, wild animals, planes, and jeeps. The clothing was shelved in crates, hung on tree branches, folded in piles on the back of a jeep. Now in the second decade of the twenty-first century, such store design has become a self-conscious category known as "themed" retailing. But in the 1980s, when most stores were selling clothes on racks and shelves inside four sterile white walls, it was fresh, groundbreaking, and fun.

In the urban street locations, the storefronts became embassies, old hotels, and colonial outposts, each store evoking an apocryphal history with crests, signs, and seals. Inside, rustic floorboards were strewn with handwoven rugs, and walls were covered with African masks, sketches, and engravings. Furnishings such as incandescent lamps, antique armoires, and zebra print upholstered wingback chairs took the customer back in time. There were often tusk door handles, caged light fixtures, shutters, stone fireplaces, and lattice ceilings with a painted sky above.

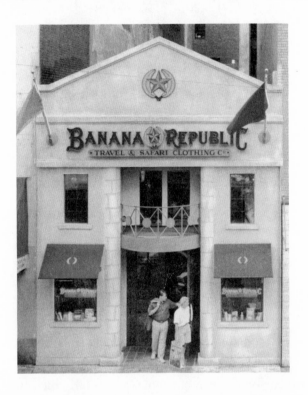

Every store, whether a tent, a lodge, or an embassy, featured unmistakable traces of an adventurous wordsmith. These included a story in progress on a slightly yellowed sheet of paper in an old Royal typewriter, located on a rock or an antique rolltop desk. Next to it were wire spectacles, a fountain pen, a tin canteen, a few coins, and a half-finished mug of coffee. And in an unabashed and shameless pitch of commercialism, the mysteriously absent writer's safari jacket could always be found hanging nearby on a tree branch or over the back of a chair.

We saw staffing as our next line of defense against falling into a chain mind-set. Whenever possible, we hired free-spirited and personable young people, particularly those who were creative or in creative professions: writers, actors, and artists, for instance. This worked not only because they were the kind of people naturally drawn to the style of the clothes but also because, given the nature of what they did for a living, many appreciated a day job. Their independent air spoke to the theme of individualism that we promulgated in the brand. In training the sales staff, we emphasized the importance of performing as local shopkeepers do, greeting and treating customers as neighbors, and participating in the community.

We expended considerable effort to keep the staff well informed so that they could be helpful to customers. The creative department produced a new video timed to the mailing of each catalogue to keep store personnel up-to-date on the lore, functions, fit, and styling of each new item, as well as to train them in how to assist customers in personalizing their travel wardrobes depending on their destinations.

The store culture reflected the company's: we were all about creativity. Everything in every store mattered—from how a collar was turned in a window display to the way customers were greeted when they entered the store. Trite greetings such as "Can I help you?" or "Is there something special you're looking for today?" were never heard. Salespeople made a sincere personal connection, if possible and appropriate, or were sensitive to customers who wanted to be left alone. Customer service? Every garment was guaranteed forever.

The staff were encouraged to share stories of their own travels. As a company, we were all about stories, visually and narratively, which inspired customers to share their narratives with us. Stores filled with fascinating conversations, as customers brought tales of their travels and told of their unique experiences in the clothes. The feeling in the stores was playful. Customers loved combining their own idea of themselves with a new idea of themselves that the clothes suggested. When a customer tried on a pith helmet or an aviator's jacket, his personal narrative might take a whimsical turn into fantasy, and the actor or writer waiting on him would be right there to join in. Besides these flights of fancy, there was always the thrill of spotting the many celebrities who frequented our stores—tacit endorsements that this was the real thing.

Traveling as much as we did and growing as fast as we were would not have been possible without Ed. A stocky man with a sweet, ineradicable grin, Ed was all action. So much action that he had no time for paper on his desk. He was always circulating throughout the company, determining what wasn't getting done right and fixing it. We could not have asked for a more perfect buffer between us and the operating side of Banana Republic. We had total confidence in him. He barked and hounded people into being smart in performing their jobs, and they were. He unfailingly got what he wanted from employees, and if he didn't, they were soon gone. His take-charge style liberated us to focus on product, stores, catalogue, and responding to a growing number of media requests.

Ed's sizable army of operational employees had a down-to-earth, analytical common sense that neatly balanced our constant invention. They could calculate how many of each item should be made in each color and each size, and which stores got what. They tracked the cash flow, the terms, the schedules, the logistics. They got the clothes manufactured and delivered, the stores built and stocked, the catalogue in the mail, the orders fulfilled, and the money in the bank. Yet they stood ready to execute every creative whim we threw their way. Theirs was a language of "price points," "finished goods," "inventory turns," "margins," and "markdowns." They were the bones of the business, and without them, we never could have expanded as quickly. As weeks turned into months turned into years, their data grew into history, which allowed them to calculate to perfection how Seattle would react to white blouses, the best way to skew the size runs in Chicago, which tops would sell best in October, and whether a given item should be expanded—and if so, in which sizes, colors, and stores.

The Banana Republic bookstores got up and running in less than a year under the direction of Irma Zigas, who had previously created the bookstore for the San Francisco Museum of Modern Art. With the exception of one freestanding store on Grant Avenue in downtown San Francisco, the bookstores were built inside or adjoining our larger existing stores. They were an instant hit. Carefully selected books about every region of the world could be borrowed or bought. We also published a separate Banana Republic bookstore catalogue.

The magazine, *Trips,* was slightly more problematic. Karma found me employing other unemployables, and it was . . . interesting. The editor I hired, Carolyn White, could not comprehend why I should have anything whatsoever to say about the magazine and the stories in it. For reasons perhaps well merited from her prior employment in corporate-owned media, Carolyn harbored a suspicion that if left to my own devices, I would pollute the magazine with puff pieces about Banana Republic. This to me was more than a little maddening, since I conceived the magazine to be independent of the clothing company. In fact, I saw its independence as its greatest merit in affirming that Banana Republic respected the intelligence of its customers—who themselves would appreciate independent journalism. In the magazine, I saw Banana Republic "presenting" first-class travel journalism, much in the way that a public television station is supported. We accepted advertising from other companies and ran some ads of our own.

But Carolyn never let go of her suspicions. Oddly, as a former journalist myself, as much as I knew she was wrongheaded, I could empathize with her caution. This time, unfortunately (but in a larger picture, fortunately), I was the moneybags, no matter how I saw myself. Nonetheless, and not easily, we worked it all out somehow, and the first issue went to press with stories by noted writers such as Richard Ford, Lewis Grossberger, Charlie Haas, and Marguerite Del Giudice. It was fearless travel journalism throughout, hardly puff stuff. In one tough story, a reporter was dispatched to the little-known and privately owned Hawaiian island of Niihau, which in some ways operated like a medieval fiefdom. I probably would have preferred not running the photo of the man with the gun at his head in a travel magazine, but Carolyn, I suspect, wanted to send confirmation to her colleagues back in New York that she hadn't sold out and wasn't producing a Banana Republic magazine-length advertorial. The inaugural spring 1988 issue, designed in digest format by the celebrated magazine designer Roger Black, was stunning.

While both businesses were revving up, Bob Fisher remained skeptical.

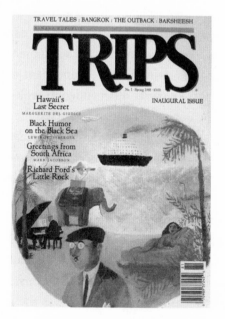

"How do we sell more clothes with a bookstore?" he asked. "What does a magazine have to do with selling clothes?"

That either would have an indirect salutary influence on infusing the notion of travel into a brand of travel clothing—adding to the brand's authority, and therefore selling more clothes—seemed to him far-fetched or, at best, fanciful. His prodding did, however, lead Patricia and me to wonder occasionally how much we might be the subject of conversation at family dinners when the clan assembled at its Sugar Bowl ski cabin near Lake Tahoe, or in Don and Doris's Laurel Heights home in San Francisco.

I had, in fact, begun to notice a subtle shift in Don's tone.

When I mentioned that the home business would be next to launch, he listened quietly without commenting and started the ensuing discussion by telling me that I reminded him of his father. When I asked why, he said his father had been a "dreamer," full of ideas, and "often those ideas didn't work out."

"I don't know about this home business," he said in conclusion. "It's best to stick with what you know."

Patricia was frustrated and disappointed, but it *was* his money, after all, and when he bought Banana Republic, it was a clothing business, not a home business. So we iced the home plans. The incident riled me for a minute or two, but then I let it go. Maybe Don was right. We were busy enough anyway with the clothing business, the bookstore, and the magazine. Throwing another business on top of all these would have strained our resources.

"Stick to what you know" thereafter became Don's refrain. I wondered if he was ever aware of the irony. What attracted him to us in the first place was our success at starting Banana Republic as professional amateurs. Sticking to what they know may be the one thing that professional amateurs unequivocally *can't* do.

We had already outgrown our offices by the time we finished the renovation in 1986. Luckily, a similar building abutting our Bluxome Street headquarters was available. All we needed to do was punch a hole through the adjoining wall to unify the offices. A structural engineer was hired to inspect the site in order to draw up the plans for a permit.

As the engineer entered through the ground floor of the renovated office building, he looked up at the newly sand-blasted twelve-by-twelve-inch wood trusses. Walking over to a supporting post, he examined the steel braces that connected the post to the trusses.

He turned to me and shook his head.

The simple matter of adding some extra office space would pivot into a series of unexpected events that would soon take the Banana Republic we'd built and tear it apart.

24

Money Knows Best

"This building," said the engineer, pointing solemnly to the ceiling of our newly renovated offices, "won't withstand a 5.0 earthquake."

This news wasn't just bad—it was havoc. We had just sunk $2 million into the renovation. The final result was a dream creative space of exposed brick walls and sandblasted wood, ten-foot-high steel windows, and a wide-open floor plan.

A 5.0 earthquake is not uncommon in the Bay Area.

I had experienced a few myself. The jolt and the roll before the shelves sway and light fixtures swing. Eerily, everything goes silent except for the books or cups or file cabinets crashing to the floor. In the next long and suspended moment comes a cascade of horrifying thoughts: Who's been hurt? Have the bridges snapped? Did skyscrapers fall? How bad are the fires? If it had been the early days, with only Patricia and me and no employees, the two of us might have been crazy enough to game the law of averages and stay. But now that was unthinkable.

"We've got to get out of here in two weeks or less," I told the managers.

Not surprisingly, we were unable to find an adequate space for a few-hundred-plus people on short notice. This necessitated splitting the company into two locations, many miles apart in the traffic-clogged Bay Area. Patricia and I moved with the creative, design, merchandising, and production staffs to a frumpy, low-ceilinged, fluorescent-lit office in a low-rise building in downtown San Francisco. The administrative and finance people went to Gap headquarters, about twelve miles south in San Bruno, where Don Fisher made space available for them.

Once we were out of the building, we handed the keys and structural engineer's report to the landlord. He sued us for breaking the lease.

Our relationship with Don Fisher remained amicable. While not reticent to send along a suggestion or two whenever he had one ("Have you thought about selling jeans?"), Don made a point of reiterating at every opportunity, "This is your company, I don't know how to run your company." In spirit as well as word, he honored the agreement we had made. On his visits, true to form, he vacuumed in as much information as he could—not only from us, but others throughout the company. Having a reporter's ear, I marveled at how well Don listened. You had the feeling that every comment was being sucked into a private data bank in his brain, to be recalled effortlessly at any time. There was little in Don's easygoing manner to suggest the widely reputed shrewd, tough businessman.

What fascinated him about Banana Republic, as he frequently articulated it, was how we blended merchandise, marketing, and design into a single story; how we named each piece of clothing and wove its tale into the company's ethos. He wanted to tie together his own stores with an idea for what Gap stood for and put it all into a cohesive package like ours. If the five hundred Gap stores could somehow catch some of the magic of Banana and move up a notch, the results could move the stuck needle on the company's stock price. After a long search for a new CEO who might be up to the task, he settled on a rising merchant named Mickey Drexler, who had recently rejuvenated Ann Taylor.

Ed knew him, or knew of him. He was uneasy.

"Watch out for Mickey," he warned us. "He's a grabber."

Before we were forced to abandon our headquarters on Bluxome Street, Don called to say that Mickey was interested in sharing some of the space there. Suburban San Bruno, where Gap was located, is only fifteen minutes away by car but light-years from San Francisco culturally. I figured that Mickey, a New Yorker, was feeling isolated down there in the industrial park cubicles that served as Gap offices. As a gesture of goodwill to Don, I might have been agreeable to letting Mickey have the space he wanted. Patricia, however, had misgivings, reinforced by Ed's cautions about Mickey's reputed unbridled ambition and wily corporate skills. I was not going to put Patricia and Ed into uncomfortable circumstances. I called Don to say Mickey's moving in was not a good idea. I explained that we were concerned that having his designers and merchants in close quarters could result in changes to Gap's line that would confuse the distinction between the Gap and Banana Republic brands. Don said he didn't see why that would be the case, but he accepted our decision.

While I had an inkling that Mickey might take our refusal to share space with him as a slight, I had a feeling he would never be a true ally anyway. As they say, good fences make good neighbors. Mickey was that rare CEO who was as involved in the product as he was in the business. I respected what he was doing for Gap. He brought everything under its own label, went for the classics, threw out the froufrou, and carved out a tasteful brand. But I felt like he was studying our game plan too closely. This attention made me uneasy. We prized our autonomy.

We did our best to cooperate where we could.

Gap was going to make a presentation to Wall Street analysts in New York, and Don asked us to come and talk about Banana Republic. The implication, of course, was that the analysts would smell a growth opportunity, which might boost the languishing Gap stock. The presentation took place in early 1987 in our largest store at Fifty-ninth Street and Lexington Avenue. The store was designed to be a colonial African home with rooms of painted wainscoting, grand stairways, and a great room with a fireplace, worn leather armchairs, and replica trophy heads on the walls. A thorn tree inspired by the one standing in the New Stanley's courtyard in Nairobi was sculpted in stucco on the facade, setting it apart from other storefronts nearby.

Before the official presentations, analysts took the time to walk around and handle the merchandise. Then they all gathered in the great room to hear Mel describe the travel theme and how it was playing out not only in clothing but also in our bookstores and now *Trips*, the travel magazine. At Don's urging, Mel told the analysts about our record-breaking sales per square foot and hinted at our extraordinary margins.

Then Mel handed the microphone to me to make the clothing presentation. Before I started, a hand went up.

"Do you see the safari trend starting to flame out? Hasn't it peaked?" an analyst near the back of the room asked.

"We don't look at it as a trend. We believe khaki has got at least the staying power of denim," Mel replied. "Also, our focus is more travel than safari, so we expect to be around for a long time."

"With your comps beginning to fall, isn't that suggesting the concept may have reached a saturation point?" interjected another analyst. "Comps," or comparable, is the term retailers use to measure sales in the same stores from one year to the next.

"No," Mel said. "But you can't expect comparable stores sales to grow double digits year after year. You can't have peaks without valleys."

"I see you're opening a new store just about every other week," said a third analyst. "How large a store base can you grow on a limited concept like this?"

"I don't see us as limited," Mel replied. "Our customers are people of all ages, men and women, teenagers to grandparents. Why don't we let Patricia talk about the clothes—you'll see why."

Before I could say a word, another hand went up:

"What effect do you think these movies like *Out of Africa* and *Raiders of the Lost Ark* are having on your sales? I know you're saying you're not a trend business, but you can't deny these movies have primed the pump, and where does that leave you when Hollywood is on to something else next year?"

"Patricia will show you why," Mel said evenly. We exchanged a quick look.

If we hadn't proven to be agile and resourceful, or hadn't at that moment been achieving more sales per square foot than any other apparel retailer in America, these might have been worthy concerns. But the narrow, hard-nosed line of questioning, plus a few questions about the catalogue business, was the *only* line of questioning that night. Cynicism gone amok. I was troubled. What unsettled me most was their presumptuousness and lack of curiosity about what made the company work. There were still lines out the door on weekends, but these financial people were fixated only on what might go wrong.

I caught a glimpse of Bob Fisher and the look he shot his father.

Later I learned that a highly regarded analyst was mulling a downgrade of Gap stock. His reasons were mostly particular to Gap, but it was clear he also saw "the Banana Republic concept" as only a "limited" rollout.

In stock market terms, the adjective *limited* isn't exactly the rocket fuel that sends a stock soaring.

When I finally began my presentation, I took the analysts through the core pieces we sold year in and year out, with only the colors changing. I showcased women's items such as the white linen blouse, pleated trousers, and featherweight cashmere sweaters. Far from trendy, these classic pieces not only traveled well but were also ideal for the office, restaurant, and most everyday occasions. I pointed out the unsized accessory line of Italian scarves, belts, and bags that now comprised a healthy 15 percent of the business, with nearly 80 percent gross margin. Also, a new shoe business that enabled us to dress our customers head to toe. I took them through the vintage-inspired leather collection, and pointed out the washed and aged fabrics we had developed. By turning garments inside out, I showed how well they were made, what a great value they were to the customer while still a good margin for us. Then I ran through the men's items in detail, making similar points. Finally, I showed the surplus items that gave customers the thrill of discovery.

As soon as I finished, another hand shot up.

"The clothes are nice—my wife even buys your things—but don't you think you might be drinking your own Kool-Aid? What's to say it's not a fad? What's to say you haven't peaked?"

Back in the Bay Area after the analysts meeting, Bob was grumpier than usual. It was no secret if you read the financial pages that the economy was stalling after a period of high growth. Gap was not doing well. Mirroring the economy, our sales too were starting to slow, particularly in cities where we had opened more than one store. The comp stores, which had been consistently growing by double-digit percentages for years, slipped to high-single-digit increases—still very good by almost any standard. Bob asked Mel if he was concerned about the comp store growth slowing. Mel said he wasn't, that expecting double digits year after year was not realistic. He repeated what he told the analysts, "You can't have peaks without valleys."

Bob asked me if maybe the "drop in comps" had anything to do with the merchandise.

"Why do we have so much khaki in the line?" he wanted to know.

"Why aren't we offering brighter colors?"

"Why don't we have shirts with button-down collars?"

Soon, I was fielding his relentless why's daily. For years, the ideas for new styles just flowed as if they were streamed in. Now Bob was running interference, distracting me from hearing the signal.

Granted, after years of autonomously planning, designing, analyzing sales, and deciding how much to order of each item, I wasn't accustomed to being questioned about trends. I had already relinquished the time-consuming, and now overwhelming, analysis required to Bob's supremely logical leadership, but it was no secret that he didn't have a feel for the product. He pushed his team to find less expensive mills and factories, which added to our margin but sometimes compromised the quality.

One day Linda Umbell, the head women's merchandiser, came to me with a production sample of an oversized women's shirt. She had been enthusiastic about the original design and the rich colors but was now worried about the fit. She asked me to try it on. It wasn't the fit that was the problem. It was that the fabric was stiffer than the finely woven cotton gauze I had designated. The new factory in Turkey, or Sri Lanka, with the lower prices had found a "close match," but it wasn't close enough to drape as well as the original, and so the shirt looked boxy and unflattering. Too late to reject, already in the catalogue, we were forced to accept several thousand disappointing shirts. This irked me, but I didn't want to make an issue about one shirt when Bob was doing his best to fill the huge demand for new merchandise.

Data was Bob's proxy for intuition. He put the store staff to work polling customers. What colors are you looking for that you don't see in the store? How much do you want to pay for a pair of khakis? Do you think our skirts are long enough? For me, this was backward. If you ask most customers what they want and how much they will pay for it, they'll tell you that they want what they have already seen and at a lower price. If you're in business to copy and knock off others, data is your designer. Our customers wanted us to create, not copy what they could get somewhere else. They had demonstrated that they understood value. When they saw a well-designed piece in a high-quality fabric, they were willing to pay for it. Even if we'd gone Bob's route and manufactured what customers when prompted might say they wanted, it would take six months for the styles to arrive in the stores. By then, it was just as likely that customers would want something else they'd just seen.

"And truck drivers? Are they our customers?" Bob asked, and had the stores poll customers on what they did for a living.

While I had at first welcomed his intellectual probings, I now found them exhausting and fruitless. I began to avoid our impromptu hallway discussions.

I didn't agree with the Wall Street cynics either. Safari-inspired was not just a trend. It was the heritage of the company. Hermès had done fine as an equestrian-inspired line for more than a century; Polo's polo ponies were still going strong. A subtle reference to safari would always be in our line (as was, for instance, sailing for Lands' End and hunting for L.L.Bean), but we were evolving constantly. The travel focus had added even more dimension. Increasingly, the clothes reflected global influences. We planned to bring the theme of a different world region into each fall and spring line to support the featured travel journal as well as to keep the line fresh. Versions of a Thai sarong, batik shirt, and Burmese cloth satchel would be featured in the upcoming Southeast Asia journal catalogue. Wool sweaters and scarves with Navajo blanket patterns, Hopi basket-style purses, plaid flannel shirts, and concho belts would complement our khakis in a catalogue with a western wilderness theme.

While Mel and I saw this planned evolution as highlighting the new travel emphasis, this too made Bob nervous. By this time, the buys were huge: as many as 100,000 of a single short, requiring big, irreversible commitments, bringing us into uncharted territory. Why couldn't we use a trend service to see if we were on track with fashion trends, Bob wanted to know, and focus groups to be double sure?

I should have realized that all the time he was spending at Gap since we had moved out of Bluxome Street had influenced his thinking. At Gap, the "merchants," as they were called, reviewed ideas put forth by designers and told them what to make. If the merchants felt an item was missing, they'd direct the designers to create it. They reached and backed up their decisions with the help of color trend consultants, fashion trend consultants, and focus groups. In the end, in lieu of instinct, the corporate culture designed the clothes. This wasn't, and never would be, our way, of course.

Our clothes were designed with input from the merchants, but design had the final say. I approved and signed off on every item we made.

Then one day, to my surprise, in a sample shipment from Italy, I spotted a leather and linen tote bag I had never seen before. It wasn't a bad-looking bag; just nothing special about it. I thought it might have been a sample made for another company accidentally sent to us. I asked the head accessory buyer if he had any idea where it came from.

"Bob felt that everyone wants totes these days, so we should sell one too," he said.

I went to find Bob. "Look," I said, "there is nothing particularly wrong with this bag, except that it's common. No details, no heritage, no character. If you feel strongly that we need an item to fill a certain category, come to me about it."

"Why? You aren't a real designer anyway," he retorted. "After all, weren't you an art major?"

Stunned by his surliness, I walked away.

The underlying problem we had with Bob was that he didn't appear to see value in creativity. He was also oblivious of the demoralizing effect he had on creative people, and I suspect unaware as well of his generally downbeat demeanor. As time went on, it was becoming a problem.

What made matters worse is that the confirmation Bob did not get from us he soon found in a new ally. Mickey Drexler let Bob know he understood his concerns about Banana, and had a few ideas of his own. Banana Republic merchandise needed to have a wider range . . . be more accessible . . . more color . . . less "gimmicky" . . .

The attacks were surreal, particularly coming at a time when we had the strongest retail and catalogue numbers in the nation, and were winning all sorts of awards—including a Cutty Sark Menswear Award, and the Direct Marketing Association's award for Best Catalogue. Later, *Catalogue Age* magazine even declared Banana Republic's catalogue to be the "Best Catalogue of All Time."

On October 19, 1987, with the company headquarters still split in two locations while new offices were being built, we decided to raise spirits by hosting a huge conference at the Claremont Hotel in Oakland. The district and store managers flew in from around the country to meet one another and the creative team. The four-day session focused on our mission, building camaraderie, and celebrating our top salespeople.

The conference could not have come at a better time, both for the company and for us. Mel and I, for the first time ever, had begun to have some doubts about our decision to sell to Gap. With Don's scenario of the-sky's-the-limit expansion, it was beginning to feel like growth for growth's sake. Although we weren't signing the leases ourselves, we were complicit in agreeing to them. Many highly desirable store locations, too good to pass up, presented themselves. By 1987 and into 1988, we were opening too many stores too fast. One day we found ourselves in a galleria that could have been Minneapolis or St. Louis or Houston, walking the upper level, passing one familiar high-end chain store after another. We looked down to the level below and saw the Banana Republic logo blinking in neon over a rusted old jeep. Yet another store we hadn't yet seen, run by a manager we hadn't yet met. We looked at each other, both thinking the same thing. How had we let this happen?

The conference brought us back. Feeling the energy of the employees, their excitement and sense of purpose, dispelled our sudden ambivalence. These were smart, personable people. We were touched by how many thanked us and told us they had never before had an opportunity to work for a company as innovative, caring, and dynamic as Banana Republic. They were passionate about the company and their jobs. When people asked us if we had any kids, Mel and I liked to say, "No, not yet—except for three thousand of them." Through the process of building the business, we'd somehow crossed over from being the kids we saw ourselves as to being "parents." But now, after all these years, a carefully guarded secret: I was pregnant. Mel and I were both glowing with happiness. A baby we'd been trying to have for a long, long time.

On the first night at the Claremont, surrounded by several hundred of our managers, all of us inside a totally Banana Republic feel-good be-smart be-happy bubble, the conference finally broke for dinner. I went out to the lobby to stretch my legs. My eye caught the headline on the afternoon newspaper:

STOCKS PLUMMET 22%
PANIC ON WALL STREET

The world had changed while we were in the conference room.

Weirdly, Gap stock telegraphed the crash when, a few weeks earlier, it missed its estimated earnings and lost a third of its value before falling by half again on this October day that would forevermore be christened Black Monday.

The country was spooked. Over the next couple of months, for the first time in our nearly ten years of business, sales flattened. Holiday sales were not what we predicted. The all-important Wall Street comparable store gauge fell into even lower single digits, and our catalogue orders also slowed. The market crash had wiped out a massive amount of wealth, and consumers were spending less of their income on discretionary items such as clothing.

In early 1988, as *Trips* was going to press, Don Fisher called me, and even though we had discussed it on several occasions, asked, "Why are we publishing a magazine?"

His question, of course, was suggesting its own answer: he was intimating that the magazine was a distraction. I explained: the magazine added to the authenticity of the brand. We were a lifestyle business. Our customers were literate. The bookstore and the magazine were to serve the customers' broader travel needs. Both also established our further authority in travel. Our clothing sales benefited from the association.

"We need to stick to what we know," he said. "I'm not sure these things are a good idea."

And then more from Bob: "How did you come up with the

women's fit? Why aren't you ordering more of the yellow and less of the green? What does Rose [Patricia's mother, who was now finding furnishings for our stores] do around here anyway? Have you guys seen what's being worn in Paris?"

There was no longer any doubt that the Fishers weren't happy.

I kept as much of it as I could from Patricia. She went into early labor and was placed on bed rest by our doctor. She worked from home with her design team, mapping out the fall line where production deadlines loomed, and relying heavily on her assistant Monica Pichler to keep her up-to-date. A month later, our baby in her arms, she walked back into the offices, and the first thing she saw were Gap people in the conference room.

My assistant buzzed to say that Don Fisher was here to see me. I had not been expecting him. With him was Mickey Drexler.

They came in, sat down, and Don cleared his throat, a habit of his, and said stiffly, "There's going to be some changes I have to make for the good of the company."

The "changes" were that going forward Patricia and I were to report to Mickey Drexler.

Mickey didn't waste a second.

He said, "I want Patricia to go to Paris tomorrow, copy the best stuff that she sees in the stores, and put together some ideas for me for the fall line, which I want by next week."

It was almost impossible in the moment for me to compute what was happening. My heart was pounding, and rage was bubbling up from every cell in my body. I looked at Don, who said nothing. Then I took a breath and looked Mickey in the eye.

"It's not going to happen, Mickey," I said.

"Fuck you, Mel!" Mickey screamed, and stormed out.

25

Coup

The astute reader will have understood, long before I, that unemployable means *unemployable*.

In many ways, it is astonishing that our adventure into employability lasted as long as it did. Until he didn't keep it anymore, Don Fisher kept his word and gave us free rein. We did what we wanted to do, and then one day we couldn't. The very idea of Mickey Drexler ordering Patricia—who had directed the design of every item Banana had ever sold; Patricia, with our one-week-old baby in arms—to go to Paris to copy (*copy!*) what was in the stores there could only have been a clumsy attempt to get us to see the door before we were shown it. So goes corporate life. One day you're in, the next day . . .

I asked Don if we could buy back our company.

"I don't sell," he said. "I only buy."

One could make a case that the fall of Gap's stock price during the time when our company was split into different locations and I was home on bed rest made us vulnerable. Mickey's hunger for respect and power, Bob's drive to be on safely quantifiable turf rather than having to go on balancing his merchandise planning on our instincts, and Don's need to keep Mickey, Bob, and Wall Street happy all conspired to make it look like it might be easier to operate the company without two unpredictable, difficult, and sometimes volatile founders calling the shots. A conversation, rather than an ambush, may have got us to the same place.

We left a lucrative new five-year contract we had just signed on the table and went on our way. The money, as much as we enjoyed having it, was an unexpected by-product anyway. All along, we had been in it for the freedom—and did we ever have freedom! The freedom to ignore convention, the freedom to imagine anything was possible, the freedom to hop on planes to explore anywhere at any time we wished, and ultimately the freedom to bring this product of our unfettered imaginations to life—all of it for no other purpose than creating the kind of company we wanted to work in. Free we were indeed. Until we weren't. When the freedom was retracted, we knew at once we'd leave.

To this day, I do not know who ordered the security guard to ask us to hand over our Banana Republic discount cards on our way out the door.

At the size the business had grown to, around $250 million in annual sales, Gap wanted predictability, and elected to believe intuition answering to data was the surest way to achieve it. Though it could have been handled with more civility, our ejection from corporate culture was perhaps the most predictable outcome of all. We traded back a future of unlimited financial wealth for what we had worked for all along: unlimited freedom.

When Mickey stepped in as president after our resignation, Ed and most of our creative staff quit. A year later, Bob took over as president of Banana Republic for about four years. The catalogue was redesigned into a slick, nine-by-twelve-inch glossy with photographs of models replacing the illustrations. The jeeps, tents, and tusks were yanked from the stores and replaced by neat white shelving. Five design teams were hired and fired. The focus on travel was replaced with fashions for "casual Friday."

Ironically, Bob, Don, and Mickey made their and the analysts' worst fears come true. As they "repositioned" the company, Banana Republic cratered. Loyal customers fled en masse. For several years, the trio found themselves explaining to analysts time and again that they never expected the sheer volume of negative reaction they got from incensed Banana Republic customers offended by the abrupt changes in the stores and catalogues. The repositioning became an apologetic "turnaround." Ultimately, after nearly a decade of thrashing about, Banana Republic was slotted, in the official lingo of the Gap annual report, into an "accessible luxury concept" with "higher price points" than Gap.

Years later, Don Fisher made another decision "in the best interest of the company." He fired Mickey Drexler. Mickey has since gone on to burnish a well-deserved reputation on Wall Street as the "merchant prince" CEO of J.Crew. Bob Fisher went on to become chairman and CEO of Gap until he stepped aside in 2007. A few years after our departure, a venture capitalist who was a mutual acquaintance asked Bob why we had left the company we founded. He declared that we were steering it in the wrong direction; that working with us was like "having an ongoing root canal." He remains a Gap director and, with his family, a major shareholder.

In 1989, the year after we left, a magnitude 7.1 earthquake struck the Bay Area just before the third game of the World Series at San Francisco's Candlestick Park. Six people were killed when our old brick building at Sixth and Bluxome streets collapsed. The landlord's lawsuit was dismissed.

Ten years after we went our separate ways, before he died after a long battle with cancer, Don Fisher spotted us at a large dinner party that he and we were attending. Cheerfully, he came over to our table to reconnect.

"I have something I've been wanting to tell you," he said with wine-enhanced enthusiasm in front of the others at the table. "That travel idea you had was brilliant. I should have stuck with it. We would have been like American Express." On several other occasions, he ran into our friend the novelist Herbert Gold at events around San Francisco. As Herb reported to us after each encounter, Don told him unfailingly, "I could have made Mel and Patricia very rich."

Very rich is not what we wanted. We just wanted to live life on our own terms. That is what we got.

When I was younger, I never found babies interesting. My only thoughts about motherhood were how to avoid it. But thankfully, Mel softened me to the possibility as I entered my midthirties. Once getting pregnant proved difficult—we battled infertility problems for years—it became another experience that I didn't want to miss. Until the moment I held our newborn son in my arms, I was expecting a baby. Now that I held him, I was flabbergasted to see that I had given birth to a *person,* a very small and young and wrinkly one, but a complete unique person no less. His eyes looked deeply into mine, and he screamed, loudly. I now had a responsibility that shrank my role as chief creative officer down to the minor leagues. I had not a clue where to start. This infant would have to teach me, teach us, how to be parents together. And we thought that starting a business was a challenge!

We turned down a tempting business opportunity from Leonard Lauder, of the eponymous cosmetics firm, to partner with him in a new venture. He introduced himself as a Banana Republic fan and customer. When he heard that we had left the company, he approached us with the idea of launching a new natural skincare brand together in which he would be the financier and we would be "its parents." We knew well what he meant when he said, "Every brand needs parents."

Meeting several times over the next several months, we liked Leonard and his wife, Evelyn. We found them both smart and gracious, and saw they had deep values by which they lived. Ultimately, however, we decided that rolling out of one business into another was not for us. In reaching our decision, we got a chance to recognize that our initial motivation for starting Banana Republic had endured and was now ready to be realized. Having started Banana to win the freedom to do whatever we wanted to do, it was odd in a loopy way to discover that the first thing we wanted to do with our freedom was *not* do another business. It drove home to us that there was not much about business that we particularly loved, even though virtually the entire world we encountered saw it differently. It was Banana Republic we had loved, not *business.* In the weeks and months, even years, after leaving Banana, the question posed to us most often was, "What's next?" The presumption was that we had to have another blockbuster business simmering. Actually, not. Never even occurred to us until Leonard came along. The Gap's Ted Tight thought he had done Don another great service in strangling us with a five-year noncompete clause in the clothing business, which we signed without a second thought. We were more than ready for a break from business.

It wasn't as much about saying no to the opportunity presented by the Lauders as it was about saying yes to a life without a title on a business card; a chance to discover *la dolce far niente*. We were fortunate to have enough money in the bank to allow us, for at least a few years, to forget about "making a living" and, instead, *live*. For perhaps the first time since we met, we were asking ourselves why, rather than why not.

When the decision was made to pass on the new venture, life was new again. I renewed my passion for yoga, started a vegetable garden, learned to cook, and took up my paintbrush. Back on the streets—well, at least on the trails in our small mountain town—I reentered a hands-on life with an infant teaching me the big joy in small things. This was humbling, enlightening, and challenging. No longer as a boss of three thousand, but as an equal, I began friendships with other new mothers who became treasured companions.

Overnight, my personal narrative shifted radically from mouthing off on "Building an Iconic Brand" to lessons in "Bringing Up Dad."

Having ascended from crawling through the wild and giddy feat of teaching himself to balance on two feet, our son was now perambulating in all directions and ready for any adventure.

We were on the porch together, and I was showing him how to catch a beach ball. I helped him to stand just so, stretch out his little arms just so, and be ready with his hands to clamp on the ball at just the right moment. My instructions tantalized him.

"Come on come on come on," he said, wiggling his arms.

"Okay," I said. "Ready?"

He wiggled his ready arms and bounced impatiently up and down.

I took a breath, looked him in the eye, and from a few feet away very gently tossed him the ball. In slow motion I saw his eyes follow the ball as it came toward him until at just the right moment his little arms reached up, and his hands clamped and held it, startling us both. Looking with awe at the ball and then at me, his eyes exploded with glee.

"I caught it, Daddy, I caught it!" He giggled with pure delight, jumping up and down.

"You did indeed, son," said I.

"More! More! More!"

I took the ball out of his hands, stepped back, and tossed it again. But his success made him even more eager to catch it a second time. He reached for the ball prematurely. It flew right past him, hit the deck, and bounced away. I made an encouraging face. He looked at me happy as ever, jumping again with pure delight, giggling:

"I missed it, Daddy, I missed it!"

The little guy had a big message. For me, it helped put to rest any residual ill feeling I harbored against the Gap pack. Yes, they could have been more gracious, but so could have we. My son was right. It was not about winning. It was about playing. And did we ever play—for nearly ten years. To us it was as much about art as business. Of course, as a toddler hasn't found out yet, winning *is* what it's all about if you are playing for points, but we were never playing for points. We were playing for fun.

Yes, we "lost" the company if you look at it through a filter of win-lose, but in reality, Banana Republic gave us exactly what we asked from it.

A lucky dad who could, I jumped at the chance to spend as much time as possible with my son. The kid, after all, had already shown me he could teach me a thing or two, as would his sister, who came along four years later. There was nothing I wanted to do more than to be Daddy. For good measure, I also took up mountain biking and body boarding, got to read books I'd always wanted to—mostly philosophy and literature. I started to paint, even tried a hand at writing a musical, delved into meditation and yoga, made it my daily goal to be present, not tense.

In 1990, two years after leaving Banana, Mel decided to try a Buddhist meditation retreat. He packed books, hiking boots, and writing pads, and drove off for ten days of silence and meditation, only to learn that reading, writing, hiking—anything but sitting in silence—were discouraged at the retreat. The purpose of the retreat was to empty one's mind, to stop thinking. With a mind that was always percolating, this was no easy task for Mel. While sitting cross-legged with his eyes closed, every time he tried to empty his mind, it filled up with a business idea he'd been thinking about since the second day he was there. He awoke that morning to discover there was no coffee. Mel experienced a caffeine withdrawal so severe that he vowed to never drink coffee again. "The black swill," his marketing mind demonized it, and . . . *voilà*! Tea was the answer. Tea was the new business idea. And once again, of course, he could be the "first customer."

The meditation was not without some effect on Mel. When he came home, he was more calm and clear, but nonetheless ready to brew a new business. As much as I loved our quiet life with time to paint and build mud castles with our son in the vegetable garden, I too got excited about building a new brand. Again it was a business wrapped in an apocryphal world, this time to market tea.

Soon afterward, Mel flew back east for a conference of the Social Venture Network, an organization for socially responsible business, where he served as a board member. On the flight back, he met an energetic and aspiring young entrepreneur named Bill Rosenzweig, who had also attended the conference. Bill managed to get Mel talking about tea for the entirety of the six-hour flight. By the time the plane landed in San Francisco, Bill landed himself a job in the new Republic of Tea as its Minister of Progress. I had already signed on as self-appointed Minister of Enchantment to help in the branding and design, as well as mixing in our kitchen the teas and herbs that would constitute the line. As Minister of Leaves, Mel conjured up the overall plan to launch the new republic.* I was pregnant with our daughter, and again consigned to bed rest by the doctor. This time I spent my days in bed thinking through my sketches and designing the packaging for the new line of teas while our son built his Legos at my side.

---

*The moment-by-moment creative process is chronicled in real time in our earlier book, *The Republic of Tea: How an Idea Becomes a Business.*

We focused on specialty premium tea, which was hard to find in the pre-Google days. In the early 1990s, if you wanted black tea, you settled for a tea bag filled with Lipton's orange pekoe dust, even in the finest restaurants. Green tea also was hard to find, and only one company, Celestial Seasonings, offered a decent range of herbal teas. With advice from our friend Bruce Katz, founder of Rockport shoes, who joined as Minister of Finance, we created a complete line of full-leaf teas.

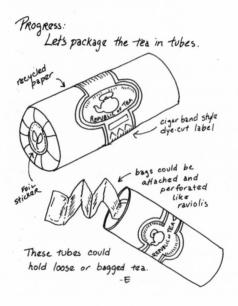

We had great fun thinking up names and descriptions for each tea. There was Mango Ceylon, "a metabolic frolic"; Assam Breakfast, "back in the body tea"; Big Green Hojicha, "chop wood carry water tea"; Ginger Peach, "longevity tea"; Chamomile Lemon, "surrender to sleep tea"; and Earl Greyer, "more of a good thing tea."

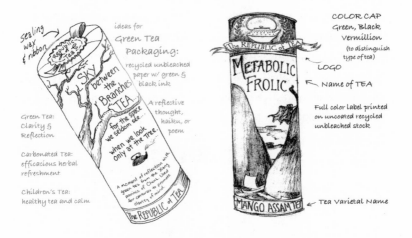

No matter how strong the concept or product was, unless the packaging stood out on the shelves and communicated the philosophy in look, shape, and feel, people would pass it by. The other brands were all packaged in square or rectangular tins or boxes; even their tea bags were square. Our packaging had to be different, but it also needed to be true. Coffee had edges, tea was rounder. So I explored round. Tins had been used traditionally to store tea, so I sketched tall, elegant round tins and even round tea bags. The art needed to be quiet, evocative. After exploring watercolors, I settled on softly colorful collages with a teapot in the foreground, celebrating the steeping process and what Mel termed as taking life "sip by sip." This phrase became the company's motto. The paper for both the labels and bags was unbleached, and the tins were refillable and recyclable. Mel's Minister of Leaves' musings to evoke "tea mind," such as "The pot gives up its emptiness for the tea," filled whatever space on the label not claimed by FDA requirements.

We launched with a line of twenty-one teas into a world of markets that allotted about twelve linear inches of shelf space to tea, and, luckily, discovered there were a lot of people like us who had been looking for a reliable purveyor of premium tea. Today the company, now in its third decade and lovingly owned and operated by Ron Rubin and his family, offers more than three hundred teas and is the prominent brand in the now twelve-*shelf* specialty tea section.

So that was the one that worked. We messed up on another one called ZoZa.

It was Ed who prompted the whole adventure. He had gone on to become CEO of Discovery Channel Stores and then retired.

He called us and said, "We had so much fun, let's do something on the Internet."

It was 1999. Venture capital firms were throwing dot-com start-up money all over the Bay Area, and some of it landed on us. These were the years when building a website that today could be built for $5,000 ran a tab that could reach $5 million—if you could find the engineers to build it. In this manic era of dot-com start-ups, much cash and adrenaline was spent on achieving "first mover advantage," which meant getting out of the gate first to build a hugely successful website in a specific category of e-commerce, such as pets, drugs, grocery delivery—or clothes. ZoZa was to be the first completely virtual clothing brand: no stores, no wholesale, our own cool clothing available only from our website. Our venture investors were entranced, as was everyone else in Silicon Valley, by the frothy possibilities of strictly e-commerce valuations unburdened by the weight of "bricks and mortar" overhead.

Our kids, then ages eleven and seven, were excited that we were going back into the clothing business, but they didn't like the idea that our new company would be only a website.

"Make it a store," they said.

Now that I was a mountain biker and body boarder, I had found that some of the natural fabrics that we swore by in Banana Republic could be wanting, even dangerous, when it came to performance. Synthetic fibers had come of age in the world of athletics for their ease of use, their functionality such as wicking moisture, their tendency not to wrinkle, and so on. Patagonia was the quintessential company for the customer who appreciated performance clothing. It had great spirit, technical savvy in materials, and estimable social values as a company, but its focus at that time was strictly outdoor adventure clothing.

Patricia was spending more time in yoga pants but didn't want to look like she was in her workout clothing all day. We started thinking that these performance fabrics could be just the thing for the rigors of everyday living. For instance, business suits that stretched, breathed, refused to wrinkle, and could be thrown into the washer and dryer. Or evening gowns that could roll up in a purse and be taken to work for an evening on the town without your having to go home to change. And they could be made from swimsuit fabric, in case you landed in the pool at the party. ZoZa was a full line of "performance" clothing for what we called "the sport of living." We had free yoga classes in the office midmornings, and a company Zen Master: my high school friend Norman Fischer, formerly the abbot of the San Francisco Zen Center. The talented Gale Parker, master of exacting fits and former creative director of Ralph Lauren's collection, joined Patricia to design a line described by the media as "Patagonia meets Prada." Actually, it was neither—just comfortable, stretchy, no-problem clothes that had a warm, futuristic look.

But as I should have remembered, the product is one thing and the business another.

In 1999, here's how the funding worked: series A got you up and running, and series B and maybe C got you to the brink of going public. Stock market valuations for dot-coms were stratospheric. If you were playing the "first mover advantage" game, the point was to spend as quickly as you could to achieve measurable results that could be used to entice round B investors at a much higher valuation. The whole thing was predicated on series B coming in.

We built the website, designed the clothes, and launched to great fanfare and a rush of business. Irrepressible retailers as we were, we quietly opened a showroom far from the center of town with samples and computer kiosks, so that customers could see and try on the clothing. A few months later, in March 2000, when the stock market was effervescing into the ether of Nasdaq

5000—*boom!* The market crashed. Series B disappeared for virtually every company that had *dot-com* in its name. It hardly mattered that ZoZa was up and running and that customer reaction could not have been more encouraging. We were out of cash, and nobody was interested in our series B. Too late, we listened to our kids and filled the showroom with our clothing, opening to booming retail sales and grossing $1 million in under six months. But we were running an overhead built to feed a monster. Even more devastating, Ed was diagnosed with an aggressive pancreatic cancer and died in a few months.

ZoZa went to dot-com heaven in 2001. We had failed to accomplish with $16 million what we had done twenty years earlier with $1,500: to start a new clothing brand.

"See," said the kids, "you should have opened stores."

A note on failure and success. The seed of success is in failure, and the seed of failure is in success. Starting ZoZa, we were probably too sure of ourselves and too hypnotized by the dot-com bubble. We trusted that if we got the product right, everything else would follow, and the company would work. We often hear from people who still wear their ZoZa clothes. They tell us with great enthusiasm and a note of sorrow that we *did* get the product right. But that's not enough. For every business, there's an appropriate scale. That one we got wrong twice.

But I'm not complaining. We got exactly what we wanted.

Today we are happy and grateful. Our kids are in their early twenties, and although they've heard from a lot of other people that their parents started Banana Republic, they haven't heard much about it from us. Kids love to look forward, so we did very little looking back. We tell this story now for them, hoping they will one day find the time to read it. We also hope our story will suggest to restless creative people everywhere that creation begins with creating the life you would like to live, without fear or inhibition. It's never a straight or smooth road, but in our experience it was the bumps and the breakdowns, the mishaps and the wrong turns, that stimulated the breakthroughs we needed to get where we wanted to go.

A special bonus for us in the process of writing: we got to do it together, and it brought back all over again how much fun it was.

Choices are hidden in the pace of the day. Intentions are hidden in choices. The desire for autonomy, creativity, being close to nature, family, and having an expansive, not hectic, life were what we found reflected back as our memories bubbled.

Since we walked out that April day in 1988, we have continued to live north of San Francisco with a mountain in our backyard where deer, fox, coyote, and puma roam.

Banana Republic feels like another lifetime. Nonetheless, people often ask if we mind seeing the changes in the company we started. Our sincere answer is that when you give up your baby for adoption, you can't quibble with how it is raised. I say this even when I read with a slight gulp in my throat that Banana Republic is opening a new flagship store on Paris's Avenue des Champs-Élysées. Since it was scale that mattered most to them, maybe Don, Bob, Mickey, and Wall Street were correct in auguring that the safari and travel theme was too limited to get the company to the $2.5 billion size it is today. It is, though, I admit, perversely satisfying to see cargo fatigues, khakis, and safari and military jackets still popular year after year.

ACKNOWLEDGMENTS

Craig Roberts and Christine Benefice, thank you for teasing the germ of this book out of us as we sailed the enchanted Bay of Islands; Robert Hardin, best pal anyone could ever wish for, thank you for the feat of remotely, from your own banana republic, helping us to fine-tune our words and thoughts; Herbert Gold for being Herbert Gold, always a beacon, dear friend, and huge fun; Bruce Katz, for your encouragement, unshakable friendship, and uncompromising truth telling; Ben Loehnen, you are an amazing editor and we hope this is not the last time we play together; Sammy Perlmutter, you are going places because you get it done; Jackie Seow, Ruth Lee-Mui, Kate Gales, Jessica Abell, Sybil Pincus, Philip Bashe, and Jim Thiel, a world-class team to birth a book; Danny Grossman for checking the work in its primitive first draft and probing it for veracity and diplomacy; Seth Godin for the generosity of your boundless imagination; Michelle Lester for your effervescent enthusiasm and keen comments; Mimi Buckley for never letting Mel forget that whatever else he was off doing, he had to keep writing; Linda Grossman, Jordana Fribourg, Chris Lopes, K.C.

Hardin—we learned something from every one of you that brought this book to its resting voice; Morton Janklow, sincere appreciation for your talents and grace; and, most important, we will never forget our coconspirators, the spirited Banana Republic employees from the grand old days, the most passionate and creative lot to ever assemble inside a "corporation"; finally, of course, to the memories of Don Fisher, Bernard Petrie, and Ed Strobin, giants all.

PHOTOGRAPH AND ILLUSTRATION CREDITS

ABOUT THE AUTHORS

Mel Ziegler is a founder of Banana Republic and The Republic of Tea. He lives near San Francisco. Patricia Ziegler is a founder of Banana Republic and The Republic of Tea. She lives near San Francisco. Find them here: www.mzpz.com.

Join the discussion about *Wild Company* here:

Facebook: facebook.com/wildcompanybook
Twitter: twitter.com/wild_company